The Sweet Life
On A
Sour Budget

Daniel Hughes

First published in 2022
Copyright © 2022 Daniel Hughes
All rights reserved.
ISBN:13-978-0-6453920-2-9

This is a work of non-fiction.

Cover design by Daniel Hughes

Printed in Australia, UK, USA and Canada by, but not limited to, Ingram Spark, Amazon KDP and other short-run POD printing companies.

Also available as an eBook

Typeset in 12pt Garamond
Further information and contact https://danzblog.com

Dedication

For: – Oliver, Sophie, Harrison, Luca and the twins Davide and Luka with no expectation they will trust my observations or find it useful until they are my age.

To: – my friends and acquaintances who provided the most inspiration and who will be the least likely to read it.

And with deep gratitude to: – Robyn Townsend for her counsel and dutiful editing, Wal Pichler for his support and camaraderie and to my Julie for her editing, interminable forbearance and patience.

Table of contents

Preface

PART ONE – HOW IT CAME TO BE	
My Friend Albert	1
The Short Version	2
The Birth of a New Life	3
The Serious Bit	4
Our Story	5
That Turned Out Well	6
Seeking the Sweet Life	7
We Can Control	8
PART TWO – SELF-CONFIDENCE	
Accidental Self-confidence	9
Judging	10
Presentation	11
Projection	12
Assumptions	13
Powerful Instincts	14
The Cat	15
Self-esteem	16
Self-confidence	17
Armour	18

PART THREE – FRIENDSHIP

Loneliness	19
The Mechanics of it	20
Selfish Friendship	21
To Friends - Of friends	22
Listening	23
On Being a To	24
Must Do List	25
Definitely Don't	26
Understand Your Friends	27
Love	28
Trust	29

PART FOUR – MONEY

Making Easy Money	30
Bucket Filling	31
Hiding Your Light	32
Leaking Money	33
Albert's Unfortunate Accident	34
Poison	35
Seduction	36
Temptation	37
The Gambler	38
Methods vs Results	39

PART FIVE – OWN YOUR HOME

Moving	40
Pride	41
Saving Up. Nah	42

A Plan	43
Build Your Home	44
PART SIX – ENJOY THE SWEET LIFE	
Albert Visits the Family	45
Pleasure and Happiness	46
Home Grown Drugs	47
Licking the Problem	48
Habits	49
Wins	50
Unhappiness	51
Negative Actions	52
The Positive Attitude Scam	53
Matters of the Mind	54
A Touch of Philosophy	55

Epilogue

Preface

The Class of 2014

"It's possible, the chance to live your life over. You can begin today."

As 2014 dawned, a group of young people were about to experience their first taste of freedom in adult life.
Just as they took their first tentative steps another group of fine 'young' men and women, born in 1949, suddenly found themselves about to retire. The members of this second group were, for one reason or another, unprepared. My wife and I were in that year's intake, the 2014 class of 'The Old and Broke'.

In my case, I had just managed to bankrupt myself, over 6 years, by wasting my assets trying to save the jobs of my employees and the life of my 30-year-old company, that had been savaged by the Global Financial Crisis. Mortally as it turns out. Fortunately, like most developed countries, Australia has a safety net pension scheme to sustain those in need.

Five years on and not a week would go by that didn't produce an interview with a 'poor old pensioner' struggling to pay the rent, terrified of eviction, anxious about the electricity bill and with no social life, living an existence restricted to watching TV and waiting to die.

We too, were still living on the Age Pension, though the outcome for us was entirely different. By then we were living in our own home, debt-free with no outstanding bills or commitments.

Three years on and we live very comfortably, extended our home, two vehicles each, with cash in the bank and full wallets. There is no hint of anxiety about bills as everything we could be billed for, is paid way in advance.

How could it be, that our outcome is so different?

~~~

Part One

How It Came To Be

My Friend Albert
1

The steam from his cup of tea disappeared in the cool morning air as the edge of the rising sun was about to appear between the crossed boots on Albert's outstretched legs. The faintest smile crossed his face as he gazed across the verandah to the wet paddocks and ghostly eucalypts to the dam and a handful of resting cattle. As he soaked up the sounds and joyous atmosphere of the countryside at dawn, a tiny surge of excitement stirred. It was Sunday and that meant just one thing, the weekly trip to Bunnings 'in the city'.

For anyone not familiar, Bunnings is by far the largest and best-known hardware chain in Australia and every regional town and city has at least one example. Albert is right, again. While Bundaberg may be considered a regional town by most of us, it is definitely a city, a regional capital to be generous.

Albert has been living a sweet life, on a very modest budget he says, since 1973 which he claims, was not only a great year, it was THE year, the best year that ever was and has never been improved upon. His dreams came to pass that year. The car manufacturer Leyland produced the P76 'with the cavernous boot' (trunk to Americans) and in Albert's opinion, it's a car that has never been bettered. It is one of his most prized possessions. His beautiful and buxom wife Neerlee Faithful accepted his proposal and he took over the family farm in Titsupp Downs.

You may be curious about his life companion, Neerlee and their two daughters who fiercely and fearlessly maintain the long family tradition of retaining the venerated family name 'Faithful' after marriage, a tradition that put them in the vanguard of progressive attitudes long before it became unexceptional, even passée in today's society.

Albert Dunning-Kruger is a man of inconsistencies and irony, both simple and complex. While intelligent, he could easily be considered somewhat intellectually stunted. His world is untroubled by the annoying nuances of shades, of meaning, feelings, inferences and concepts. The world exists in the three primary colours which is good enough for Albert. He considers shades of colour, or shades of anything else for that matter, an unnecessary extravagance.

Albert doesn't have a computer. He reckons all this 'new internet craze' is too complicated. He pre-fixes everything dated after 1979 with the word 'new'.

Albert's life is a series of sole-purpose missions, carried out with care for his fellow creatures, good humour, great confidence and clarity of purpose. He could have been Forrest Gump's dad, at once dumb as, and brilliant too. That is the beauty of creating a family from scratch, an author can be as wilful as can be.

Albert is not only my greatest fan, as if that alone is not enough for me to love him, but he has much to teach us about the absurd world in which we live, as he deftly handles life with the tools, the lessons and the wisdom, the rest of us take a lifetime to amass.

As we progress through his favourite book, the very one you are reading now, we will catch glimpses of the life of Albert and his family as he tells us, first person, about his day and perhaps something of his wisdom, a sliver of insight into his unfathomable mind.

The reality of my years post Global Financial Crisis is nothing like the life I have created for Albert and his family.

~~~

It's December 2012, 4.15am and I'm jangled awake, not slowly, calmly, drowsily, but instantly jolted, fully alert, the creeping fear enveloping me.

The stabbing pain in my chest announces the re-start of battle, as it has every ghastly morning for the last two years, a deadly fight against the destruction of my life.

I dress and leave, taking nothing but my office keys and the thought that I'm one step closer to the death, the destruction of my life and with it, my 30-year-old company.

Fortunately I not only survived, it's a war I ultimately won. The pain subsides eventually, I push through the stress and start to think about how I'll find enough for the worker's wages and where I may find a lifeline.

For six years post the 2008 Global Financial Crisis I fought with every dollar, every asset, every ounce of my now obliterated pride, to save the business, but eventually it will be to no avail.

The millions that passed through my hands over the last 30 years are no more. I am no more, my company is no more and the fear of failure, all consuming.

Albert doesn't give up easily and neither do I, but eventually there comes a time.

~~~

The Short Version
2

"You can't trust quotes on the internet." – Mark Twain.

Like many things attributed to Mark Twain, he is supposed to have said in a long letter to a friend, that he apologized for its length, but he did not have time to write a short one.

Whether he first said it or not, it's true, brevity is more difficult. This is a very short book, considering there are a great many things a man or a woman can learn in a long lifetime, so it has taken much longer to pare and edit than write, more than I would have liked.

The irony is that all that wisdom and experience is mostly only useful after one has lived it. 'You can't put an old head on young shoulders, blah blah'. Alternatively, I suppose one could write it down and let someone younger take advantage, if they chose to that is.

Why take it to the grave? Why not tell my grandchildren and yours (and you for that matter) what I've discovered, how a man or a woman can become successful, even on a limited income? I've done just that, built our new house on nothing more than a government pension, but I've also earned millions and employed hundreds of people, so there is a broad perspective here.

"But why" you may ask, "would I put our success story, our journey from destitute to home ownership on a meagre income, at the beginning? After all, isn't that what a reader wants to know? How we did it?"

It is true that a reader may just want to know how we got from bankrupt to home ownership on a pension in five years but that is unlikely to be of much help and probably difficult to replicate unless one has an identical history, knowledge, skill set, work and life experience.

Living a sweet life is SO much more than owning your home, although there is no doubt, home ownership comes in as number one goal.

There are many pieces of knowledge that together, make it possible for someone to accomplish a sweet life, using their particular set of skills. In addition to the infinite variety of skills and experiences, there are innumerable possible paths to take, but the basic tools are common to us all, so this book is really about highlighting the underpinning knowledge required. With that in hand, one is best equipped to map out one's own path to a sweet life.

What IS a sweet life and how important IS owning a mortgage-free home? It seems to me to be one lived with sufficient resources to sustain your needs and much of your desires in the absence of anxiety. Of course that answer seems simple enough, you don't need to own a house to be happy and isn't that what we mean by living a sweet life?

Consider this perspective. If you don't own your home, can you ever truly rule out the anxiety that one day, you could be out on the street? The answer then is probably that you can lead a moderately-good to very good life without owning your home, but the most security and reduction in anxiety only comes with total control. As long as you can contribute your share of the cost of running your community via your taxes, in most countries, those with a robust rule of law, home ownership provides the foundation for living without fear.

Home ownership alone of course, will not be a panacea, a single solution to achieving a sweet life but it does provide the foundation.

I was not the only one surprised by the ease of doing it. It seems logical to think there must be luck or other forces at work and yet it did not seem to me that our attitude or skills were so different to anyone else. Then it began to dawn on me that we could not have done the business, if we didn't have that bit of luck, good health (I thought) and some minor skills and experiences that made it happen. But what exactly were these so-called 'skills'?.

One possibility is the absence of major medical issues but between us in the first three years, we worked through a hip replacement, a broken collar bone and a broken arm. And that's just Julie. For my part there was the triple bypass operation and then the 'open him up again' operation to fix the dodgy wire that held my chest together and a few construction accidents, a wayward steel roof truss that tried to kill me, falls from ladders and other minor bumps and bruises.
No, I don't think perfect health is the primary cause.

My next possibility is motivation. Maybe we were just more motivated to improve our dire circumstances, but that does not hold up to scrutiny either. Motivation is founded on knowledge. A crude example: if a seemingly unmotivated pensioner found out that someone had buried a gold nugget in a patch of dirt in the garden, they would be highly motivated to get the shovel out of the shed. So no, motivation is not the answer but it does lead us back to 'skills' or more accurately, knowledge.

Knowing how to conjure up money and acquire the assistance and cooperation of many people, would be a distinct advantage, I thought. With that in mind, I determined to write down the subjects about which I have acquired at least a basic understanding. I then split them into two lists, 'interesting, but yeah' and 'this helped me'.

As insignificant as some things appeared, many contributed in some small way. To my mind, these are not special skills, just the basics, albeit acquired over a long time and it seems, they helped produce the result we wanted, our own home and freedom from anxiety.

While the short story of how we came to be living the sweet life may hold some interest, the important characters are the non-de-script. Separately, they are ordinary, but together, they seem to have combined to produce a wonderful outcome and this book talks about many of them.

Once complete, frankly I was astonished that such a disparate bunch of subjects could be so connected, so intertwined that served to provide me the tools to achieve the result we wanted. I was totally oblivious to the contribution of each.

As you glance through the chapters, I expect you too to question, how many of them could possibly be connected to living a sweet life.

How could chapters on friendship, love, gambling, serotonin, appearance, selecting real estate, trust, dopamine, philosophy and my imaginary friends possibly have in common or contribute to our beautiful life?

And that's just some of the chapters. There are many others, equally puzzling. In each, where possible, I will try to show the connection to living a sweet life

~~~

The Birth of a New Life
3

"It's a serious financial health hazard."

After I accepted defeat, that my company, my assets and my life's achievements were gone, the days were more than a little grinding, incredibly stressful and emotional.

Nonetheless, this was no time for self-pity, a lot of decisions had to be made, principally among them, finding a place to live.

Rent is a financial health hazard, so the first matter to attend to was obviously having a place to sleep and so the small camper, the best we could afford, was exchanged for Julie's car, as you will read about shortly.

We had known for a long time that rent is poison. Just as tobacco is to physical health, rent is to financial health. Sometimes you can't avoid the smoke, sometimes you can't avoid rent, but it must be banished as soon as possible.

At our age, to put together our own home and a sweet life while paying rent was impossible. Had we been younger, perhaps it could have been a short-term burden to endure, but when you have a limited time ahead to get the job done, there was no way to even consider it.

With that in mind and the fact we had no dependents, we discussed several possibilities. Our first choice was to attempt to spend the next few years living in other people's houses, where we would be comfortable and still able to save. This was the house-sitting idea.

Second choice would have been moving to the country and exchanging some light labour in farm work, for accommodation. Many country businesses also struggle to find reliable workers. Accommodation would still likely be satisfactory.

Another idea was to move to the gem fields and try our hand at fossicking but that seemed a risky strategy and finally, instead of the camper, we could buy an old boat and live on that. As we had considerable experience living onboard, this was viable but limited our opportunities.

These were the main alternatives to renting that we discussed. As it turned out, our ability to show that we were trustworthy and reliable, provided us with 34 or more house-sitting opportunities, back-to-back, across 4 states. We were able to live safely and comfortably and do 'holidays' at the same time.

I am sure that this would not have worked, had we not appreciated the other, seemingly unrelated subjects in this book.

We could not have won over the hearts and minds of our new friends for whom we were able to guarantee a worry-free holiday while we looked after their home and pets, had we not spent an enormous effort in writing the perfect introductory letter. They would never have had the chance to know us, learn of our great fit for their circumstances, if they never got past the first few lines.

Grammar, punctuation, construction, attention to their special desires, I re-wrote and refined our introductory letter more than 50 times. We agonized over just the right photos to include with each application. Many of our competitors made no such effort, shooting off hundreds of form letters, most of which were thrown in the bin.

I hadn't thought much about the contribution of good communications until I began to analyse how we came to claim our sweet life. We had so many offers, about a 90% success rate, against on average 30 other applicants, it was important that we did not burn bridges so time was put into managing all the possible homes, locations and contact details in a spread sheet. We even had to create a humble 'thanks and decline' letter, we had so many offers. If I hadn't already been familiar with spread sheets, a short course in how to use them would have been necessary from the start.

Being organized is a critical skill in getting your act together. It takes discipline to record every important detail, account numbers, passwords, account names, dates of actions, places, people, future contacts, details and more details. Add dealing with years of bankruptcy to the mix. We tend to take the easy path and say "I'll remember that" but we never do. We have a whole section of the book devoted to just this one skill.

Another seemingly small skill that played a grand part was the art of selling. A lot of the book has been devoted to this critical art and it appears in just about every section. It may not be labelled 'selling' but that is what it is.

Consider this less as a book and more as a longish letter, by necessity cut to just the essence, the short version.

I guess this is my opinion about the things that gave us the chance to live a sweet life, despite a less-than-optimal start. I hope many of these observations will be of use to others and especially useful to you.

~~~

The Serious Bit
4

"The purpose of our lives is to be happy." – Dalai Lama

Albert, my imaginary friend, has all the ingredients necessary to live a sweet life. As I imagine him, he was fortunate, living in a seriously pleasant country environment, in sound physical and mental health, he also possessed the attributes that we CAN control. Not everyone is so fortunate and briefly we need to identify the serious bits and identify the parts you will need to address so that you too, can enjoy the sweet life.

I'm not a serious guy. I'm nearly always happy, these days anyway and I don't take life too seriously. I guess this is the serious chapter. There has to be one, best get it over.

Once we are past this one, you can relax and we can learn a lot together, about ourselves, our friends and lovers, about lovely things, like money and owning property, the sweet life. We may even get to hear some of Albert's stories.

Controlling or offering advice on solving the three vital factors — a safe environment, moderately-good physical health and untroubled mental health — are beyond the scope of this book. We are therefore, not setting out to fix these three issues, but we will briefly identify them and make some suggestions that might help.

A Safe Environment

Many countries are essentially safe to live in, where one is safe from the government, war, the military, the police, armed gangs, insurgents, terrorists, religious fanatics and war lords. Most of us live where guns, violence, drugs and rampant crime are minimal, rare or non-existent, where at least some basic income, healthcare and age or infirmity welfare is guaranteed.

As the majority of countries are essentially safe and well-run, the blame for most, not all but most, unsafe environments is rightfully laid at the door of domestic violence, control or domination.

It's true there are other forms of distress, verbal or physical abuse or bullying by bosses or colleagues, psychological impacts of mental impairments like bi-polar and other illnesses, poverty without the knowledge or ability to change, insecurities from poor upbringing, literacy issues and more.

It is also true there are parts of a couple of suburbs in most large cities where crime is prevalent and yes, the homeless are vulnerable to predation as are the customers of drug dealers, but nothing compares to the widespread, hidden malicious malady of domestic violence.

Aside from desperate remedies, both legal and not so much, time and distance provide the best protection. Many would consider the risk, the difficulty and the injustice of being forced to move, worth suffering in exchange for a shot at living a secure life. I can think of no better advice.

The point is that if you are in a bad situation and there is any possibility of moving, with or without support, then it is better to face the uncertain future with hope, than staying and suffering a future with no hope.

The situation is more difficult if you are an individual in a toxic relationship and you have concerns about being tracked and punished. You will definitely need to plan your escape and seek alliances and legal protection as far as possible. There are specialist organizations who can help you but you must resolve to get away and take advantage of the help that is out there.

Take heart from the experience of many who have successfully torn themselves from such misery and gone on to successfully raise their children and lead secure, happy and fulfilled lives.

Physical Health

The concepts, the ideas in this book should not be taken as exclusively for those who have many decades in front of them. Enjoyment that begins now is just as satisfying, no matter how much time you have left on your ticket. This is obviously very difficult if not impossible for someone living with chronic pain or sustained illness.

Despite uncomfortable circumstances, many people appreciate not just parts of their lives but are pleased just to be here to see, feel and absorb much of the beauty around them and I stand in awe of that strength of mind.

Mental health

Mental health in incredibly complex so my contribution is limited to asking you to think about whether you have issues that may need to be addressed while working on the steps you can take to improve your position.

Unless you have been extraordinarily lucky, at some point you have been betrayed, misled and unfairly treated. Most of us have been the victim of Kafkaesque (mindless bureaucratic) decisions by big business or Government that unfairly and worse pointlessly, affect us in a very negative way.

Being let down, tricked or misled by a partner, trusted friend or a relative is not uncommon and neither is the realization that life in general has treated us badly. We feel that through no fault of our own, we will now never be in the financial or social position we hoped for, the position we were promised. These tend to foster a general distrust of people and they are realized, they materialize, as resentment.

Chronic resentment is probably one of the few mental health issues that can be addressed without professional help. This malady is a real happiness killer and its fertile soil grows only one weed, self-pity.

The sufferer believes, justifiably in many cases, that someone else is responsible for their unfortunate circumstances. It may be true that someone else is largely responsible for the decisions that led to the current situation so at first glance, the treatment is counter intuitive. The most effective treatment is that the sufferer takes all the responsibility for their circumstance upon themselves.

The logic is that if one accepts all or most of the responsibility, whether entirely justified or not, the brain enters a mode that puts together the understandable reasons for the failure, it justifies the failure and though one did their best in the circumstances, 'bad things happen'.

If it helps to know, to some extent at least, this is true as we all have opportunities, we all make decisions, we are all responsible finally for our own happiness and circumstances anyway.

If you are angry, you will fail at living a sweet life. If you cling to, recall and relive the hurt that has been done to you, you will fail. If you often think about the slights and insults, the injustices, the sheer unfairness of life, you will fail. There is no amount of money, no home good enough to fix anger and its child, self-pity.

Alternatively, you can starve self-pity to death. Put resentful thoughts out, ignore them, change the subject, eventually they will stop bothering you.

With that more pleasant mindset, one chokes off the supply of resentment to self-pity, which is an ugly social look anyway. Self-medicating for this malady should take the form of getting a tiny fire hose and blasting self-pity out of every nook and cranny, every crack and crevice in your brain.

Now that we've acknowledged the gritty bits that are hard to influence, let's get down to the business of dealing with all the other fun bits you can control and I hope you will find it as useful as did I.

~~~

Our Story
5

"Life is to be enjoyed, not endured."

If one had the temerity to consider writing a book about enjoying a sweet life on a sour or modest budget, avoiding the dumb mistakes (or 'growth spurts' as one wit described them) he or she had better have some broad experience to back it up.

My first question with this ambitious thought in mind was, do I have the experience with a wide range of people, lifestyles, employment, finances and other matters to undertake such a task? Even considering the possibility that I may be a little biased, I think I do, but you will decide.

It is primarily with this in mind that I grit my teeth and do one of the things I dislike most, talk about my life experience. It is my natural inclination to avoid self-promotion and as I have such an aversion to braggers, I struggle to write about my life at all. Self-promotion is not my strong suite. In the end I decided it is better to validate the foundation upon which this book is set and our story is included solely for that purpose.

~~~

Julie and I have lived as a couple, two and a half times longer than we lived as individuals so it comes as no surprise that the words 'my' and 'our' have come to have the same meaning for us. We met in Sydney in 1970 and we were sure, we would be retired at 40. Life was easy, we were young, good looking, enthusiastic and capable.

By the age of twenty-three, we had moved interstate and I had taken over as the youngest branch sales manager for one of the major life insurance companies, recruiting and training sales staff. I had lofty expectations for my future. Uncomfortable with supervision, at age 25 I gave up the corporate game and started a small handyman business which I sold a year or two later and founded a glass company.

Still not sure what I wanted to do with my life, I closed the business upon the urging of friends and joined them in managing hotels on behalf of one of the breweries. Again the chaffing of supervision became too much and after concluding I was not good employee material, I founded my second glass company that was to keep me busy for the next 30 years.

Not so busy I had time to indulge my imagination, other occupations in which I could dabble, while staff kept the business ticking over.

Julie meantime was working on her own career eventually buying her own house after taking early retirement as a fleet manager for the Federal Government's Department of Administrative Services.

The decision

July 2007 was the time of a fateful decision. Business was going well, construction was booming and we had the experience and knowledge, winning several high-rise building contracts. The glass business is so machinery-dependent, to get to the next level, you either have all the machinery or none. There is no 'in-between' so you can't just ease up. We took the million-dollar risk to go into debt to install a huge furnace and other processing machinery to make hardened glass widely used in high rise buildings as well as glass pool fences and shower screens among other things. There was only one company in the city with this capability and it seemed a good idea to share the market and reduce our costs at the same time.

We had no way of knowing that a national company and competitor only a few kilometres away, had the same idea, or that the Global Financial Crisis was just around the corner. Our million-dollar toughening plant was commissioned on the same day as our new competitor and the city now had three plants instead of one, an unfortunate and dramatic oversupply.

In a construction market obliterated by the GFC and a massive oversupply of manufacturing capability, a year later we were in some trouble, but we struggled on, determined to save the company, our future and the jobs of our workers.

We had made so much headway it looked like we would survive our wounds. To keep afloat, every cent, every asset we had accumulated over the previous 25 years was put into bringing more diverse machinery on to the manufacturing line, expanding our capability and market, reinventing the company as a double-glazing manufacturer.

Soon we were shipping product across the country. The operation was largely financed by a handful of investors who each contributed the equivalent of about a year's wages, together with distribution rights sold to companies in other states. Just as it looked like the gamble had paid off, in 2011 another milder downturn struck and by 2013, our now 30-year-old company was at death's door.

My Worst Offense. The Sunk Cost Fallacy.
There are many concepts in this book that are useful and will help you enjoy a sweet life but there are a few items that are downright dangerous. So dangerous, I am talking about saving your life and I don't mean medically, although it could apply even there.

The 'saving your life' I want to discuss is rescuing it from being wasted on pointless exercises. Also known as 'cognitive entrapment', 'chasing losses', 'come this far', 'invested so much', 'can't stop now' these phrases describe one of the most destructive thought processes that infect our minds.

In a long string of offences against the Sunk Cost Fallacy, like a gambler (perversely a pursuit I dislike intensely and for which I have nothing good to say) what nearly killed me was the sunk cost fallacy.

Like a gambler chasing losses, I was consumed by the concept that I had invested so much, I had been working my entire life towards building my business, there was no way I was going to give in now.

After the GFC, the future was no future and the truth was staring me in the face, calling my name, repeatedly showing me there was little to no hope of saving the company, but still, for six long, intensely stressful, unhealthy years it was 'I've come this far'. It was stupidity on steroids.

The uncomfortable truth I had to face was that, despite my conceited idea of my objectivity and science-based decision making, I was a victim of the sunk cost fallacy. In my case, what was worse, I had devoted decades of my life to building my business on the worst of all scenarios, rented ground.

Despite the business making millions of dollars, employing hundreds of people, principally because I was very good at making the sale, engendering confidence, capable of learning new skills, an innovator extraordinaire, there was never enough profit to achieve the most basic goal, owning one's own land and premise.

Essentially, I had started in the middle, building the business, not at the beginning, which was to avoid rent like it was poisonous, which it is.

I don't want to appear didactic or arrogant, giving unsolicited advice but I guess I am going to. If you happen to have been in a business for a long time and you are not totally independent, debt-free, living a sweet life, leave now. Not tomorrow, not tonight, now.

It is a significant contributor to the early death of pilots, captains and leaders, taking themselves and their charges to early demise on the basis that we must persist in travelling this particular course.

There is nothing, no downside so seemingly bad, that it is worth losing the precious gift of a sweet life. Yes people will talk (for a day or so then forget you existed) yes, people will have to find other jobs, yes, you will have to face paying back debts, yes, you will have to find another income, BUT you will live with the chance to live a sweet life. Better to **live** any way, than **exist** in misery, a life that will lead nowhere but to more misery.

To a significant extent, this applies too if you are persisting in a relationship that clearly has little prospect for long term sweet life. Choose another path. You are presented with dozens every day and choosing one that is not the one you are presently on will not guarantee a sweet life, but staying on the current part WILL almost certainly result in a less than happy life.

Am I happy with the **direction** (improving financially year on year)?
Am I happy with my**self**, my enthusiasm, my joy in life?
Am I confident my relationship, if you have one, is now and will continue to be, a joy to be in?

If the answer to any of these is 'no' then my recommendation is to select one of the hundreds of paths offered to you. No matter what minor path change you take, it will soon show signs of heading in a new direction. If you like that direction, look for other paths that seem to be going that way too, but above all, get off the path you are **now** on. This is a part you can definitely control.

Every day we are presented with paths to follow, with no idea of where they will lead, governed by what we so glibly call 'fate'. What we mostly do, is choose between the path we are already on and what appears to be, an even easier path. In the main, we take little regard for what should be our purpose in life, the long-term goal of relishing every moment of every day.

Now that I've saved your life, you're welcome, we can talk about what happened when I chose another path.

~~~

That Turned Out Well
6

I finally accepted that my efforts had been wasted and there was nothing to be gained by even thinking about it.

Early 2014 brought relief. The company was dead but I was alive, no longer working from 5am to 6pm 7 days a week, no longer waking at 4am with stress chest pain, but penniless. Our investors lost a year's pay from their investment portfolio, we lost everything, houses, cars, motorbikes, boats and the other assets we had expected to enjoy in retirement.

To add to the pain was the guilt of having let down our investors and the companies and individuals who bought the rights to our system. It's a stabbing pain that often still wakes me at 4am all these years later. Knowing there was nothing I could have done to prevent the disaster goes no way to assuaging the remorse.

The future
We had no money, no assets and no home, which could be seen as a little troubling. Strangely, I felt no depression, quite the opposite in fact. I had just survived

six years of intense, gut-wrenching stress and witnessed my life being destroyed.

I was allowed to keep a few things, my old work truck, so I had transport, a few tools, a little cash from the sale of our personal household goods and my small retirement nest egg, equal to about 3 months wages.

Through no fault of her own, the bankruptcy was expanded to take down my wife Julie, so her assets including her house, were also forfeit. She had only her car and some small savings, a few months wages.

We needed to get back on our feet and paying rent was not an option. We sold her car and bought an old Nissan campervan so at least we had somewhere to sleep. Obviously living in the camper was not suitable long term so we decided to do the only thing possible, go on holidays. I figured we were due.

I always knew, life is a barter. We use money to measure our success, but in the end, what you receive is in proportion to the size of the benefit you deliver. It could be a big benefit for a few or a small benefit for many. With that in mind, I knew there were a lot of other people who wanted to take a holiday but were constrained by the golden handcuffs of gardens, pets and home security.

We had no such impediments, so we joined an on-line house-sitting site and advertised that we would look after the garden, the goldfish and Fido. For the next three years we travelled the country, living in some wonderful homes and on farms, paying very little, which was good because that's what we had.

We were able to live rent-free with brief periods between using the camper in free camps, which are spread across the country. Initially, we had no income as I was still a few months shy of applying for a pension.

We were like teenagers again, positive, full of energy and for the first time in 44 years together, we had no responsibilities. With only a pension to sustain us, for three years, we travelled across 4 states and drove 50,000 kilometres.

We paid no rent, no electricity, no gas and no pay TV. We lived in villages, towns, regional cities and three capital cities, two farmhouses, two shops, thirteen houses, six very nice houses and one mansion.

We ran an ice cream shop, did light maintenance repairs to beach side homes, lived on suburban allotments, five-acre allotments, twice on mountain tops, once on an island and twice on thousand + acre farms.

We loved, absolutely loved, that time in our life. The stark contrast between the misery of watching the company die and the freedom of the open road, made us the happiest we have been since we were young.

Our shortest stay was two weeks, our longest three months. We drove modern cars and 4-wheel-drives to take home-owner's fur babies to the beach and for sightseeing (ours, not the fur babies) all the while living in some mighty fine accommodation.

In more than half the cases, I had a man-cave workshop to use as my own. Since the day of our bankruptcy, we've dressed in the best clothes, often with designer labels by shopping at the charity stores.

Every homeowner invited us to use up whatever was in the fridge as it would be spoiled anyway by the time their holidays were over and to help ourselves to the produce from the garden. Our costs were reduced to our mobile phones, the occasional bottle of wine and fuel to the next destination where we would meet our 'about-to-be' new friends.

Great memories are forever ours, gazing at the stars on a crisp spring night in a sky unpolluted by city lights and humbled by a primal forest. We walked the last bridge in Australia and at the end of that road, sat on a deserted beach and gazed across The Great Southern Ocean to Antarctica. We picnicked along world class scenic rivers and breathed the cleanest air in the world.

The city lights and view over the mighty Tasman bridge from our up-market house in Hobart, stood in stark contrast to the village pub we admired from across the street the week before.

It was a joy to spend a few weeks in the beautiful village of Derby with the Ringarooma River behind, where I watched a platypus go about its business, oblivious to my presence on the bridge above.

Spending a day on the Sydney Harbour ferries, travelling the backroads to follow the Southern Australian coastline, camping by the ocean on a full moon were counter points to the glitzy lights of the world-famous Gold Coast from our (temporary) home on the mountain above.

~~~

Seeking the Sweet Life
7

Bad news and good news nearly always come together. Our good fortune, the good news in which our bankruptcy was wrapped, was that it occurred close to my retirement, which is not an intuitive conclusion. Nonetheless, it meant we were entitled to a small retirement pension although at the time I did not realize the size of the income was less important than the balance between income and expenditure.

The acceptance of our circumstances, the reality that we could not afford to pay rent inspired the house-sitting solution. Had we not been forced to cut our expenses, it is unlikely we would have enjoyed three of the best, most enjoyable, dare I say, happiest years of our lives. Sitting around lamenting the loss of one's life work, one's treasured business and assets serves no benefit to anyone.

As we had no rent to pay, by the time three years had passed, in 2017, we had saved enough to start thinking about building another house. We had the good fortune to stumble across a quarter acre in a village of just 80 houses, a morning drive from the State capital with a clear running small river at the end of the street. Down the road a few kilometres there is a boat ramp with access to the sea 20 minutes downstream.

Given our circumstances, Ray, my impulsive youngest brother, wanted to gift us the land we discovered. He went ahead and bought it on our behalf but, although deeply touched by his generosity, we managed to convince him our still untouched combined retirement money would cover it, but only just. We started building a house with money we had saved, supplemented with a gift from him.

After the slab was poured it became obvious that I would need heart surgery and a triple bypass fixed the problem. Three weeks later I was back for an 'unzip' operation to replace the wires that held my chesty bits together. Six weeks after that I began, slowly, laying the concrete blocks for the walls.

We searched for free stuff and accepted any gift of unwanted furniture or building materials we could get. I found a cheap demolished shed online and with some help and a hired truck, got it home to our block. The components were enough to build a roof that complied to cyclone standards, with some additional steel support added.

Within two years, by Christmas 2019, the house I started was signed off by the local council, completed in just five years from the bankruptcy, financed largely from the Government pension.

We have a home debt free, so financial management is not difficult. We would not have learned that a low income does not mean you can't have money left over, money you don't need to survive. What we learned was that you need a reliable income, no matter how small, you need to cut your expenses to be 20% less than your income. That provides the foundations to build on and once we had that, we took to it with a passion.

This story might evoke from you a "yes, but...." that you can't build your own house and don't have experience doing small jobs and .... To be fair though, you are probably not old and bankrupt either.

We were forced to face an apparent death-knell and learned that my obsession with earning more money was wrong-headed. We just needed a steady income and coupled to that, we made reducing our costs a way of life, an artform we came to enjoy and still do today. I had finally learned that I did not need a multi-million-dollar business or a sparkling career to be happy.

Now our lives are full of contrast and we have endless options. We would never go back to our former life, an endless uphill cycle of earning and spending.

Be the one who accepts how things really are, have the courage to act and at the end, have fewer regrets. If you do that my friend, I will have achieved a worthy goal.

~~~

We Can Control
8

"You will always be more disappointed by the number of things you didn't do, than by the few you did."

There are a few things that make it easier to achieve a happy life and they happen to be the ones we can control or at least strongly influence; self-confidence, friends, income, surplus cash and a debt-free home. Even better if you can wangle a relationship, some community connections and a half-decent family.

This is a brief word about each and I'm not claiming that living a sweet life is impossible without all these things, but we'll have a crack at the lot.

Self-confidence
This is fortunately within the grasp of all. For most of us for example, the thought of speechmaking or group presentations makes us more than just uncomfortable, indeed it can fill us with dread. You are not alone if the mere thought of making a speech encourages an inconvenient bowel movement. You may not believe that you can ever be truly confident, but I will show you

how you can achieve that goal.

Friendship

Epicurus was a smart guy, one of my role models, even though he died more than two thousand years before I was born. He did not subscribe to the notion we are here for a 'purpose' but suggested a contented life is a worthy goal in its own right. He suggested it should be lived as simply as practical and achieved free of fear, pain, anxiety, suffering and the shackles of superstition. Radical thinking for his time, his school was open to women and slaves. He thought they were as entitled to happiness as anyone. To Epicurus, friendship was a very important part of a successful life.

He said *"of all the things which wisdom has contrived which contribute to a blessed life, none is more important, more fruitful, than friendship."*

He thought that our existence is incidental, of no consequence to the Universe, that any purpose is one we invented and that supernatural belief arises from fear of our inevitable death (an existential nihilist). It made sense to me and I decided to take his advice.

We tend to think of people being in either our 'friends' group or our 'acquaintances' group. The real difference is that people come in two distinct flavours, basically two different groups and each group will contain both friends and acquaintances. We are going to classify your friends in a way that you have not done before.

Excess Cash

Excess cash is not money you can throw away, it's money in your wallet, in the bank, that is not needed for your sustenance, not needed to pay bills. When you've lived a while with spare cash, going back to week-to-week living is like, getting kicked off social media, for some a thought too horrible to contemplate.

A debt-free home
Sure, if you are severely mentally or physically disadvantaged, this goal is a struggle you may not win, but for most people, owning your own home may not be as difficult as you imagine. You just need someone to show you how and the determination to act on the advice. You do that and you WILL own your home.

A Relationship
A warm relationship is a subject discussed endlessly on social media and I do not intend to weigh-in with romantic advice. Well not much anyway, however when you read the chapters in the 'Friends' section, think about how this advice might apply to the acquisition of a take-home friend. Good to have, worth pursuing, not essential.

Community
Some people live a long, contented life moderately isolated from the rest of society and find the idea of being involved in the community a marriage of fingernails and blackboards. As with the relationship advice, if being part of the community appeals to you, consider my words about friends in the following chapters and see how it could apply here too.

A half-decent family
Nice to have if you are lucky, but nothing anyone can do about it. You can't change other people, you can only

change yourself so if you have terrible relations, you are always going to have them. Fortunately, they are not a critical part of your happiness.

~~~

Part Two

Self-confidence

Accidental Self-confidence
9

If there is one controllable factor for a sweet life that Albert has in spades, it's self-confidence. Albert's full name is Albert Ian Dunning-Kruger, or Albert 'idk' which is a rather interesting coincidence.

While many of you may know social media shorthand, not all are familiar with Albert's surname and this might be a good time to put it into your browser. The discovery of the source of his name may shed more than a little light onto many of my dear friend's attitude and unusual view of the world.

My friend Albert and his wife Neerlee (who maintains the family tradition of retaining the venerated maternal name 'Faithful' after marriage) live on a small acreage at No.1 Old School Lane, Titsupp Downs. They drive their trusty 1973 Leyland P76 with the cavernous boot (trunk to Americans) to town every Sunday to visit Bundaberg Bunnings. Mr. Dunning-Kruger knows that he is smart and savvy. He is neither.

Strange as it may seem, there are people who are supremely confident for all the wrong reasons. You are probably not one of them.

There are good folk, like my wonderful friend, who simply do not know that life can be full of embarrassments and this might lead us to the conclusion that self-confidence is the absence of fear of ridicule, criticism or embarrassment over mistakes made.

If one is blithely unaware of their blunders, what is to be embarrassed about? Why would one not feel self-confident?

It may not be going too far to suggest the more intelligent, the more aware one becomes, the more one understands lack of self-confidence. Any lack of confidence you may feel could indeed be a reflection of your superior intellect and understanding.

I think Albert's recounting of his Sunday visit to the hardware store sets an example to us all. Dear friend as he may be, it's one I'd rather not take.

This is what he told me, this afternoon upon his return.

~~~

"It was another beautiful Sunday morning in Bundaberg. As you know, I like to support local business and some guys in a few local businesses told me the best way was to take all my questions to Bunnings as they had plenty of spare time. And that was their job.

It was quite sunny out except for the clouds, so Neerlee Faithful and I drove into the undercover parking area (the building down the back with the 'trade' sign outside). I noticed again there is no parking space for my 76 Honda 7 hp CT110 Postie, not that I'd have time to make it all the way from Titsupp Downs to town on a Sunday, but I must take that up with management one day.

We got there early (9.30) to miss the crowds and straight away found a Bunnings lady who had three customers on her tail. I knew she would appreciate my intervention so I bailed her up and asked where I could find the firewood. "Ask Old Diamond, inside" she said, what I thought sounded a bit desperate and she gestured her thumb towards the auto doors before scurrying away with her gaggle of customers trailing behind, looking for all the world like a mother duck.

I had no idea who Old Diamond was but the moment we got through the doors, I saw the only one who could possibly answer such a description. The beam of light that bounced from the ceiling off his head was indeed like a diamond and he certainly looked old, maybe older than me.

He looked at me, sized me up, with one of those looks reserved for guys who got a battery drill for Christmas and are looking for somewhere to use it. It's my fault, I forgot to wear my discount shirt. For those who may not know, you can get a hiviz shirt with the stains already embedded from the Salvos for a few bucks. Anyone seeing you in that expects that you will expect a trade discount and sometimes don't even try to get you to pay retail. That's why they're called 'discount shirts'.

Anyway, I asked Old Diamond where I could find the firewood and he suggested maybe down with the BBQs, which are located near the Bunnings toilet. For those of you who are familiar with the Bunnings layout, the Bunnings toilets are a long way from the Bunnings Trade doors and I didn't bring my morning tea. Not that I'm suggesting I wanted to eat my morning tea in or around the toilets but with my knees, by the time I got back it would past my morning teatime. I asked him for an alternative.

He looked at me funny and I had to glance away from the light that was sparkling off his head but he said, "well, we've got a very nice selection of bolts and screws in the next aisle". I thanked him but thought better to go onto my other purchase, some railway sleepers.

Now I had his interest and he leaned forward like we were having a conspiracy and said, "go back out the doors and ask Kenny at the boom gate". He then went on, "but be a bit careful because he has just had an organ transplant and while some reckon it was above his shoulders, I'm pretty sure it was below, so, you know, it's probably his heart". "I think you should make a lot of noise walking up to him, you know, not to startle him. Just in case".

With that good advice in mind, I hurried out the automatic trade doors and stomped up to Kenny, who looked at me with a baleful eye and said "somethin' wrong with ya boots?" I said no, I just wanted to know where I could buy some railway sleepers. "Railway sleepers?" he repeated and I said yes, a friend of mine bought some recently to make lattice and I wanted to try it. "Make lattice with railway sleepers" he repeated.

I don't know why he kept repeating what I said, maybe to cement it into his mind, but I went on, hoping he could keep up "well, he's got this big saw and he cuts them into wafers and then he cuts….." I trailed off as I could see he was no longer with me, gazing out through the doors towards the airport, with a faraway look. I reckon he was thinking about other ways he could be spending his retirement.

Neerlee and I left him to it and heading into town to visit the Bundaberg railway station. I'd ask the Stationmaster. If anyone knew where I could get some railway sleepers, it would be him and you know, he's got plenty of time. And that's his job."

~~~

You see what I mean by Albert's enviable self-confidence, but I suspect he comes up short in the next chapter.

~~~

Judging
10

"…. but then, I think rain is wet, so who am I to judge?" – *Douglas Adams.*

One of the foremost skills your ancestors had to learn was how to read or 'judge' people, a term which has taken on a bad inference lately, becoming synonymous with criticism, especially when expressed in social media. We are constantly scolded by internet social 'experts' who think that 'judging' and 'criticizing' are synonymous, that 'you shouldn't judge people' as though you have an option.

While my imaginary friend Albert is not big on judging people, I suspect actually that he sees people the way birds see cows and tractors, large moving objects that often stir up opportunities.

For the rest of us, being able to accurately judge people, evaluate people, is essential to survival. It is not possible to avoid. You do it many times a day, whether you recognize it or not. Your ancestors happen to have been rather good at it, for which you should be grateful as one small error of judgement and you would be history, or rather, not history, or anything else. You would not exist.

Judging people means interpreting their appearance, mannerisms, speech and movement and making critical decisions based on that judgement. Failure to do this accurately, used to be fatal. Today you may be merely ripped off, cheated or ignored.

Twelve thousand years ago, the earth entered one of its short warm periods known as the Holocene. It is 'short' in geophysical terms so it should last another 20,000 years or so if we don't stuff it up.

We have been around as a separate species for about 300,000 years and until relatively recently, shared our lives with several other human species.

Homo Sapiens, with their oversized brain, were quick to capitalize on the absence of freezing their tits off by discovering control/farming of other animals and plants.

This provided the capability to feed more family members and alleviated the need to spend all their time finding food. About ten thousand years ago, the numbers grew so rapidly, villages, then towns and cities formed. Bear in mind, this was just 400 generations ago. Before that your grandad was chasing small animals with a stick so grandma would be nice to him.

For two hundred thousand prior years, our circle of acquaintances, was made up of a handful of friends and relatives, a neighbouring tribe of enemies with whom we competed and perhaps traded and others we could call the 'doubtful'.

These 'doubtful' may have been friendly, maybe not, but assuming they are friendly is not a mistake one would make too often and survive. Those who made this mistake, those who did not develop the useful art of judging, did not survive to produce you. No, your ancestors handed down the finely tuned instinct to distrust strangers and keep them away from you, your family and your possessions.

As our recent expansion took hold, our circle of 'doubtful' individuals grew at a pace much faster than our previous 200,000 years of evolution prepared us for. Today, we are surrounded by a few friends, a few enemies and tens of thousands of the 'doubtful'.

The ones we 'know' in the modern world via the media, are still processed with the same ancient mental tools our ancestors used and as a result, we assign the 'friends' tag to those who appeal to us based on their presentation and the glimpse we have of their private lives.

We have many powerful instincts and if we wish to go against them, we must deal with them at an intellectual level. We are often instinctively motivated to act a certain way, but it is contrary to our modern lives so we are forced to deal with it on a conscious level. For example, we are prone to racism, due mainly to the instinct to be wary of strangers although today it is totally unnecessary, not to mention a very bad thing to do to someone who has done you no wrong and is merely from a different group.

As far as judging people is concerned, do not be put off by social media busybodies, who have no idea how many times a day they judge people and who have even less idea how critical it is to our journey. Do not allow the disagreeable feeling of being judged to cause you to try to avoid judging others, this is misplaced compassion. You simply must judge people and you have no choice anyway. Your ancestors saw to that.

We should not try to restrain our instinct for judging people as there is no prospect for success and restraint opens us to an increased probability of harm or exploitation. That said, this is not a license to criticize those around us.

On the contrary, it should serve as a reminder that our judgement is not infallible and giving others the chance to show they have the potential to be friends, is an intelligent way to deal with your judgement of them.

If people had judged us badly, our journey to the sweet life would have been delayed or broken. Understanding judgement and its place in your life is important.

A good example of the consequences of being too friendly is the reception received by the bumbling incompetent Christopher Columbus. In the highlight of his limited career he stumbled upon an island in the Bahamas just two months and 6,000 kilometres after setting sail to encircle the globe, which was rather larger than he imagined.

Not big on details and not sure where he was, he described it as having "very green trees and many ponds and fruits of various kinds" which is why no one else to this day knows where he landed either.

He set up a camp in Haiti, the country occupying the western half of the island of Hispaniola and recorded "They brought us parrots and balls of cotton and spears and many other things, which they exchanged for the glass beads and hawks' bells," he wrote. "... They were well-built, with good bodies and handsome features. They do not bear arms. They would make fine servants. With fifty men we could subjugate them all and make them do whatever we want."

The charming Signore Columbus did just that, forcing them to look for gold and building a settlement. He sent 500 slaves to the Queen who was horrified and sent them back, mainly because if he had 'discovered' them, they were technically Spanish citizens.

By the end of his third failed voyage, he was arrested when the Queen discovered his 1200 troops had killed all but a few hundred of the quarter-million Taino native population. A 'thankyou' for the warm reception.

He wangled a 4th expedition but wrecked two of the four ships and went home in disgrace. (He named the people 'Indians' going to his grave convinced he had sailed to India, which in the direction he was going would have been another 30,000 kilometres via South America, New Zealand and Australia. He never managed to set foot on mainland Nth America to 'discover' it and anyway two million people already lived there, so the whole 'discovery' idea is a nonsense anyway.)

Presentation 11

"If you want to be judged in a certain manner, be sure your look and demeanour give that impression" – **Richelle E. Goodrich**

It's not humanity's best trait, an unfortunate one, but we are treated, initially at least, according to how we look. For many people, this is not a helpful start and for others, life is just a stroll in the park. Unfair, but true.

As we know, Albert learned this lesson early in life and as his recent trip to Bunnings showed, he knew his presentation was lacking by the absence of his 'discount shirt' so Old Diamond treated him with mild distain.

If I had to pick just one of the dozens of subjects we will discuss, I could easily choose this one as the one with the most potential to make or break your journey to the sweet life.

We could be forgiven for thinking that our 'presentation' is merely our appearance, that the way we were born governs our appearance and there is little we can do about it. The truth is that some of us are born with a face only a film director could love.

In fact, we only need look to the film industry to see the frailty of the idea we can do little about our appearance. We've all seen a director create menacing characters from the most innocuous subjects, children, dolls and architecturally challenged houses. Using expressions, music, inference, lighting and other tools, something or someone can have their projection, their character utterly and dramatically changed.

This shows us that presentation is much, much more than merely the appearance one was issued at birth, that presentation is far more than mere physical attributes.

I am convinced that my clear understanding of the importance of presentation was a major contributing factor to our success in moving past the bankruptcy disaster. I knew for sure, that how we were received by our potential hosts, the ones who would hand over their homes and pets to us, would determine if we had a free roof over our heads, which in turn allowed us to save a lot of money that would have been wasted on rent.

Yes, presentation is vital to achieving the sweet life.

Have you ever sat in a coffee shop and watched people passing by, guessing what they are like, where they come from, their social status? Have you tried to guess if they are rich or poor, perky or sad, friend or foe? It is a favourite pastime for many even if some of the sights could scare The Terminator. It's true, 'you can't judge a book by its cover' but still we try.

What you are looking at is their overall presentation which is their basic layout, provided free mainly by their parents' fumbling in the dark, overlaid with the factors they control, clothes, hair, makeup, adornments, body-fat percentage and facial expression. Less obvious but nonetheless informative is gait, stance and movement.

There are things about your appearance you can't change. If you have a face like a bag of bricks, it's not going to be your greatest asset. Obviously, looking like a Brad Pitt or a supermodel is going to open a lot of doors, so yes, your basic layout is a strong influence, but you control a significant part of that, maybe 60% and 100% of the rest so overall, you are 80% in control. I'm taking a few liberties with the numbers but you get the point.

If one were motivated to try it, you could on just one day, meet five people for the first time and create in each an entirely first impression choosing from *confident, arrogant, determined, crazy-dangerous, to happy, sad, scared, harmless, and dozens of others.* Each person you met would have an entirely unique perspective about who you are and none of that takes into consideration your physical appearance.

A group of men or women of similar age, weight and features could stand chatting in a room and you will be able to guess, fairly accurately, which is the confident one, the introvert, the extrovert, the nervous, the shy one and many other more subtle clues to their personality.

After they speak a few sentences, your impression

strengthens and as they speak more, it reaches a plateau where you have made your final assessment, one that is unlikely to change much no matter what they say from that point on.

Important point
Interestingly, at the first meeting, people generally accept whatever you deliver as true. People will believe just about anything you put forward. It's not a chance you're going to get again so worth taking a little extra care.

It's comforting to know that we are totally in control of the first impression and most of it is not controlled by that fateful DNA swap with sweet nothings whispered so long ago, that led to your reading this page.

That first impression affects the willingness of others to open the door to you. If people are reluctant to give you a chance to show your talents, to demonstrate what you can offer, it takes a concerted effort to get them to listen and accept you.

How can you have the essentials, ready cash, a home you own, things highlighted in the introduction, if you don't have the opportunities? How can you do these things if no one will give you a chance?
We know it shouldn't matter, but how you look **does** matter, **especially to you**, because it has a massive effect on how your life is going to turn out and this is why it does. When people look at you, they are assessing your current and **future usefulness** to them and the level of threat you present.

~~~

Projection
12

Regardless of how uncomfortable the thought makes us we must accept that we are mostly assessing others for their usefulness. So is everyone else.

If the appearance that nature provided is less than extraordinary (and let's face it, that's most of us) we then need to learn how to exploit the adornments and express the non-visible to our advantage. Making a good first impression gives us the best chance to show what benefits we can provide and our friendship is the best and cheapest service we have.

When you are meeting someone for the first time, consciously or otherwise, the ones you favour are the ones most likely to give you the most value, be that entertainment (a 'fun' person) a service (help with a project or problem) or a life partner. What we are unconsciously assessing is the future value in each other.

Regardless of your age, the way your life proceeds from this point, pleasantly or painfully, is totally, utterly dependent on your ability to project your future value.

Fortunately, you get to control it and how you project it. The people in your life who have future value to you include partners, friends, friends of friends, tradesmen, co-workers, some or all your extended family and these are naturally, the ones to whom you gravitate and are also the ones for whom you are prepared to do the most.

In the beginning, it was my job to show homeowners, that knowing us was a huge benefit. They could take a holiday with peace of mind which was incredibly important to them. It was crucial to our success. Our ability to project our future usefulness is still important of course, but in different ways to different people.

We tend to ignore those who have little future value to us, the nodding neighbours, the old, the bland, those who don't physically appeal to us and the children of our acquaintances. In short, it's those who are merely peripheral in our world.

If, in your private, honest thoughts, this rings uncomfortably true for you, you might feel a slight prick of conscience, however you should not be ashamed. You were bred for this. You have strong instincts pushing you to assess, score and secure those who appear to be useful to your survival and your ability to produce more mini-mees. This kept your ancestors alive to produce you, so you should not be too critical of yourself or others.
Someone who always seems pleased to see us, always has a smile and a joke, always seems to enjoy their life, they

are attractive to us. Why? The answer is that they are **future useful**.

When interacting with a happy person, there is negligible risk of unpleasantness, danger or embarrassment. You feel welcome and your opinions seem to be valued. These people seem to have lots of people who are pleased to see them. They have more 'friends' depending on what you think are 'friends' which is a whole other subject which we will address shortly.

You may not feel particularly joyous in every moment, in every interaction you have with friends but that does not stop you from acting that way. You are projecting your future value as someone who will always be welcome because you are useful. You bring a smile, reassurance in a sometimes-unwelcoming world so of course you are useful.

There is a side benefit too, for some reason, when we act a certain way, we quickly begin to feel that way for real. Spooky or what?

When Julie and I kicked off our new life and embraced the opportunity to live our lives over to some extent, one of the most important things we did was to ensure our presentation gave us the best shot.

In our profile picture to prospective homeowners, we picked the one that looked the youngest (within reason) the most vigorous, the friendliest, most welcoming image we could choose.

We are genetically disposed, as are all other creatures, to

look for the best partner to make more little creatures just like us and to achieve this best outcome, we look for the most attractive partner who will have us. At breeding age, we all go through an all too brief period when we look the best, our presentation is vibrant, the most attractive individual we will ever be. In that brief period, most try to pair up and this is the time when you have the best chance of getting a good deal. (I know you had a single word ending for that sentence.)

The trick is to advertise the future value, to take up the opportunities while making it clear you are not there for the taking. That provides control of the flow of benefit and what is demanded in return can range from a fantastic job, good contacts, friendship or a closer relationship. It is up to the individual.

As youth fades, alas so quickly, we need to learn to produce and project a lot more future value, to manage diminishing desirability, diminishing present value. Most do this by enhancing potential earnings, strong partnership contribution and/or the ability to produce healthy offspring.

No matter how good or bad your physical presentation life is largely dependent on your future value. This never changes, even into your dotage. This cannot be overstated.

Regardless of your age, the way your life proceeds from this point, pleasantly or painfully, is totally, utterly dependent on your ability to project your future value.

The act of projecting your future value should always be

a priority, towards the ones we care about and to the public at large. The consequences of failing to do this can be painful.

~~~

Assumptions
13

The lesson of Presentation is that it alerts us to the uncomfortable fact that we will are judged by our looks, somewhat unfairly you might say.

In this short chapter allow me to introduce you to one of Albert's family, his son-in-law and his best friend.

Meet Tall Terry
Albert's family is well, different. What one would expect of an imaginary family.

Albert and Neerlee Faithful have two daughters, Offin and Canbie Faithful who follow the tradition of keeping the venerated maternal family name 'Faithful' after marriage. I'll tell you more about Offin Faithful later but suffice to say, she is married to Tall Terry who isn't. (Tall, not not married.)

Like her sister Canbie, she carries the Faithful maternal gene that necessitates the wearing of XXL blouses and also, like them, is the beneficiary of a 'small-waist' gene.

This has been passed down the maternal line from their great-great grandmothers, who inspired the invention of the corset, which they didn't need but apparently their great-great grandmother's friends felt that nature had failed them somewhat in that department.

Offin's husband, Tall Terry Tucker who isn't and who owns a few acres next door to Albert, could most easily be described as one of the true gentlemen truck drivers. In appearance Tall Terry is more geometrically related to a cube, rather than a cylinder. He may not be tall but he is wide and he is thick. Not that he is stupid, far from it. Like Albert, he knows he is smart and savvy.

Tall Terry has a lot of hair, indeed a vast amount of hair. Unfortunately, none of it is on top and he is so rectangular, when he's standing still, his head looks for all the world like a smooth river rock on a tombstone.

While the top may be scant of hair, south of that anatomical feature where most of us have a neck, Tall Terry has what some unkind person might call, a pelt. But Offin loves him. They were childhood sweethearts.

Tall Terry Tucker's head is so bare and patterned with dents and scars, Albert sometimes has to stop and look a second time to see if Tall Terry is coming towards him or walking away. His hands look a bit like hubcaps and his fingers look like they've had one too many losing battles with his semi-trailer's dog chains.

Tall Terry's good mate is Toad Agin, also a truck driver

trading as 'Agin's Transport'. Toad has a proper first name, but nobody has ever been game to ask. There is a story that Albert, Tall Terry's father-in-law was going to tell Toad that it seemed unkind to call him a 'toad' but Tall Terry pointed out the wisdom of keeping schtum on what could be a sore point.

While Toad's mother, who sadly passed away, some say from shame, admitted she could have tried harder in the looks department, Toad is a kind and wonderful friend, provided you don't mention the origin of his name.

Toad has often been mistaken for a brother to Tall Terry. Rumour around Titsupp Downs has it that Toad's mum was a very friendly person, as was Tall Terry's dad, a man of short stature but very game, apparently. When Tall Terry and Toad are standing side by side, they look for all the world like a low, badly painted Besser Block wall.

Unfortunately, Toad has never been able to afford a decent truck, which he finds embarrassing because it keeps breaking down. Every time the tow truck drivers have to come out, the radio is alive with chatter, like "don't tell me he has to be Towed Agin?" And that's how he got his name. Best not associate his looks with 'towed'.

The lesson: don't make assumptions about people.

~~~

Powerful Instincts
14

"We are driven by instinct to seize opportunities created by weak defences."

When an animal, including our own species, sees something of value in a weakened or defenceless situation, instinct kicks in and it is motivated to take advantage.

I want to think that my imaginary friend Albert is exempt from this unfortunate aspect of human nature, but I know, deep in my heart, we are driven by primal urges and it takes a massive effort of will, to tame these instincts. At least, let's get acquainted with them and understand why it may affect us.

I feel especially fortunate that I had a clear understanding of this chapter long before we were forced into penury. Without understanding the powerful instincts that drive us all, I would not have been able to pull off the trick of getting us back into the black in such a short time. I strongly recommend understanding this next chapter.

Acquisition
The acquisition instinct is moderated naturally by the potential penalty incurred in making the 'kill'. All animals evolved to react to a helpless or weakened animal with a primary 'acquisition' attack to obtain/store food. In humans this expanded to include invading the lands of others, stealing their possessions, subjugating or taking advantage for sexual gratification and it's not one of our endearing traits. The 'acquisition' instinct is one of the strongest prime instincts and survival depended on it.

Five and a half million years ago, the rising landmass that was to become Panama, cut off the ocean interchange between the North Atlantic and the Pacific Ocean, diverting the flow of hot and cold ocean currents. Our pre-human ancestors in Africa were forced onto the savannah by the change in moisture-bearing winds, which caused a massive reduction in forests.

Later, when your ancestors, who evolved from these human precursors, roamed these vast grass lands and they came across a helpless animal, those that seized the chance to kill it and share with family or store for later, are the ones who survived to breed you.

That **'acquisition'** instinct is as strong in you today as it was say, two hundred thousand years ago, or even one thousand years ago. In the absence of human development in ways we can't guess, it will probably still be strong many thousands of years from now. Prime instincts are extraordinarily slow to change.

The main primal moderator of the acquisition instinct is self-preservation, so any animal that appeared to have strong defences was to be avoided unless there was a pressing need. The weak and defenceless can be attacked immediately with confidence.

Nurture

The 'Nurture' instinct overrides the acquisition instinct on certain occasions for obvious evolutionary benefits. A species that kills their own helpless young is not going to last long. This nurture instinct arises in animals that produce young that need care and who would otherwise kill and eat them. They have no compunction about eating the young of others of course.

Occasionally presented as a curiosity of nature on social media and popular video, this instinct misfires when a sated predator 'nurtures' a newborn prey animal, rather than act on their primal acquisition instinct.

Allies

The 'Allies' instinct is another that can override the instinct to acquire. Sometimes also called the compassion instinct, it arose in herd animals. For social animals like humans, this compassion or 'allies' instinct led to the benefit of having more soldiers to defend the tribe and to add to one's group of friends and protectors. This has been extended to members of one's larger social group, after villages evolved 12,000 years ago.

In modern society all three instincts, acquisition, nurture and allies are evident every day. If you are vulnerable due to age, financial constraints, physically or sexually vulnerable, disabled or in a minority, you will certainly experience at least some degree of discrimination or acquisition, taking advantage of one's vulnerability. In many cases, people only restrain themselves to treat you with respect and do things for you out of fear of the consequences.

The Vulnerable

The most disturbing aspect for the vulnerable is the number of times the 'acquisition' instinct degenerates into a self-gratification exercise of power, played out as domestic violence. These cowards attack or exercise control when they think there will be no consequences. Power often runs amuck when these instincts are not moderated and there is no fear of retribution, wielded with disdain for and disinterest in the debilitating effect on others.

Some societies, less progressive and some would say less 'evolved' still resist the self-evident concept that women are not possessions, that women are equal to men. It also manifests as male domination of daughters, controlling every aspect of their lives until they are sold on with an agreed bride price to the 'care' of another male in an arranged marriage.

Willie Nelsen

There is a story, acknowledged by Willie Nelson but not necessarily complete or accurate in detail after being retold so many times, that after a severe transgression against his first wife Martha, she sewed the drunken Mr Nelson into his bed one night. Whether he had attacked her or just severely annoyed her we may never know, but her alleged subsequent actions served to make a point. Once he was helpless, so the story goes, she woke him and then set about beating the immobilized offender with a broom handle.

There is little doubt this beating would have been on his mind for quite some time after the event and would have given him more than a little pause for thought had he contemplated lashing out again (if indeed that WAS the transgression).

'Accidental' discrimination

Outside this widespread overt and deliberate exploitation of the weaker individual, there is 'accidental' or more accurately, ignorant and uncaring predation whereby the aggressor is blithely unaware of the hurt they are inflicting.

This often plays out as casual racism and discrimination where the offender is quite unaware or inured by habit to the grief he or she is causing. Unfortunately, many times the offender is well aware of the hurt but makes no effort to desist. Those of us who allow this to pass without comment are by default, complicit in this aggression as everyone present recognizes the aggression is taking place and our silence is effectively endorsing the act.

There is nothing inside this shape which is why it's called 'negative space'. It's created by what's not there rather than by what is, but the shape is unmistakable.

Those among us who have no particular concern or interest in the poor, the immigrant, minorities and subjugated women, probably do not see themselves as biased, bigoted, misogynistic or racist in any way. Ignoring or tolerating this behaviour though, is the same unmistakable shape, the same size and is felt the same way as overt, biased, bigoted and racist actions. It matters little where your sense of right and wrong come from, the absence of demonstrating concern for others has the same effect as clear biased, bigoted or racist actions or remarks. If not exactly the same effect, at least it gives a damn good imitation of it.

It's a salient point that this form of attack seldom takes place when the attacker suspects their target is capable of inflicting pain upon them or when they may be chastised by the group.

For anyone suffering at the hands of these uncaring cowards, understanding the drivers and frequency of these instincts is useful to construct defences. Obviously, the best defence is to avoid getting into a defenceless position in the first place. When this is not possible, the best way to avoid exploitation is to avoid advertising or drawing attention to vulnerability.

Unfortunately, this too is often not an option. How you deal with your vulnerability and construct good defences, we will now investigate.

~~~

The Cat
15

"Cats find humans useful domestic animals" – George Mikes

Imagine you are locked in a room with a cat, one you suspect is not in a good mood. You know perfectly well that you are bigger and more powerful, yet you sense some fear. Claws and teeth tend to inspire that.

What you fear is its **potential**. You respect what the cat can do, so you treat it with caution. Even though your power is the greater, still you fear the cat and that is not entirely because not so long ago, we were just lunch for his larger cousins.

(I've just remembered, Albert's wife Neerlee used to have a cat. Sad case, it might get a mention later.)

Defences
The cat always looks neutral in disposition, mostly expressionless even, but it never looks vulnerable and it takes a determined individual to overcome their fear of the consequences to attack one. Like the cat, if you do

not appear to be vulnerable and show some latent potential for harm, most people will not be tempted by their 'acquisition' instincts to take advantage of your situation.

There is no point bemoaning the facts and being angry that people are not 'better than that'. The point is that people are just another evolved animal with old, deeply imbedded instincts that are difficult to counter.

How to deal with limited defences
If you need a product or service and have little money to pay for it, don't waste your time playing the 'defenceless but lovable' lamb. You will be screwed almost every time or at best, patted on the head and told to go away. Most times the lions kill the defenceless whether they are hungry or not.

Sure there is pity, humans have the capacity to pity the defenceless, however even if you are prepared to accept pity, don't depend on getting it. Few have much to spare and most are secretly pleased to see you in an inferior position as this enhances their position relative to you.

When your vulnerability is unavoidably evident, the best defence is to disguise it as far as possible and/or falsify/deny that you are vulnerable. To achieve this, the best method is to advertise strength instead.

As we have already discovered, many attacks, or in other cases, being ignored, come from inadvertent wounding words or actions. If you appear as though you have the power to cause pain, be it physical, emotional, financial or social, the 'acquisition' instinct is less likely to fire up, averting the need for them to have to deal with at an intellectual level.

Most unfortunate detrimental 'attacks' come from those who are not consciously acting on their 'acquisition' instinct. **If you are vulnerable, the best defence is a combination of appearing to be capable of inflicting pain and offering the possibility of reward by future value.**

Ensure you do not look or say anything that promotes or suggests your vulnerability to avoid having to battle the other person's 'acquisition' response. Be the cat that just wants to be friends, albeit one with sharp teeth and even sharper claws.

You need to be careful when showing this capability as it can also present as a challenge which can trigger a reaction of putting you in your place. You must position yourself as a nice person who just wants to get along but one who is capable of inflicting pain if necessary.

Appeal to their 'allies' instinct.
Surprisingly, despite a very thin argument or how tenuous the possibility of your future benefit to them (as a future customer or goodwill ambassador for example) many will ignore their scepticism to 'justify' to themselves foregoing their 'acquisition' instinct.

Don't linger once they have agreed to the 'ally' proposal. Get and go before they change their mind as the 'acquisition' instinct is strong and it can be turned on in an instant.

If you are not well-off financially, discuss it only in terms of its being **a short-term problem** and mention the way in which the other person **will benefit from your future prosperity.** If you are physically disabled, only talk about your **future power prospects,** which could be a possible financial gain, powerful allies you already have or new strong allies joining you shortly and or influence that could benefit the other.

Clearly, we are not all the same but many people tend to measure a man or woman and value their opinion in direct proportion to their wealth, position or how famous they are. Why the opinion of a moronic movie star should carry more weight with a significant part of the population than the opinion of a respected professional, is the subject of much educated speculation.

For our purposes here, it doesn't matter why. Knowing the reason or reasons will not change anything. Perception is everything.

In the year 275 BCE ('before current era' previously known as BC) Pyrrhus, the king of Epirus, took on the Romans in southern Italy. He was skilled at war and had a powerful army fortified by war elephants (which the Romans were not experienced in facing). Pyrrhus won the first two battles but suffered heavy losses. Pyrrhus said "If we are victorious in one more battle, we shall be utterly ruined." This has come to be known as a Pyrrhic Victory.

When negotiating with a more powerful person or entity, you can still win. The message that will give you the best deal is when the other party believe victory over you will cost them more than the victory is worth, that is, a Pyrrhic victory.

There are many ways in which power is expressed and while I am not suggesting or recommending you use some or all these tools, it's best if you recognize them. Nevertheless, there may be times when you need these tools to protect yourself.

Financial: Intimate or at least keep secret the extent of your power to buy muscle and influence.
Contacts: Claiming influential friends or relatives (strong allies)
Disruption: The power to cause large scale inconvenience
Exposure: The power to expose others to scrutiny or public ridicule
Embarrassment: The power to cause social scenes
Instability: The fear of someone being aggressively out of control or influence

These are but a few expressions of power, of potential pain, causing hesitation, uncertainty and influencing how you are treated. The mere hint that you are capable, can in many cases, curb ill intentions.

~~~

Self-esteem
16

"No one can make you feel inferior without your consent."

Before you can feel genuine self-confidence, you need to have self-esteem, you need to be proud of yourself. You also need to know the difference between pride and self-esteem.

To quote Bruce Lee, legendary martial artist, philosopher and filmmaker (1940–1973): ***Pride is a sense of worth derived from something that is not part of us.***

To clarify, 'not part of us' includes the physical appearance we inherited. If you are proud of yourself because you are pretty or handsome or because of your house or car or your family's money, that is pride. Pride creates a fragile façade of confidence, one that can crumble at any time if it's seriously challenged. The stereo-typical oversized bully has a fragile self-confidence derived from an inheritance, bulk usually and often in the absence of an adequate IQ.

This does not mean that having pride is wrong. You can justly have pride in the way you act, the way you dress,

your city, your team and many other things. However, we just need to realize that pride has a dangerous side as well. For example, you can have justified pride that your team won the grand final and still have pride when they are losing,

although by then your emotion is more likely loyalty. Loyalty is a whole other bag of eels we won't open here but it develops from either trust or faith, which are two matters we will address a little later.

Be aware that pride, when taken beyond rational feelings, can develop into emotions like tribalism, nationalism, patriotism and others that can bring out our less than charming side.

While it may appear obvious that one needs to have self-confidence to really enjoy the sweet life, perhaps we forget easily that our self-esteem is equally important.

During a long life, there were times when my self-confidence was wavering, thin and exhausted but I don't think my self-esteem was ever threatened. I always felt I had power over my weaknesses.

Self-esteem comes from the exercise of power over oneself.

This is easily accessible to all by the simple practice of gratification postponement. If you routinely put off taking easy pleasures in shopping, eating, drinking, outings and other short-term pleasures, you are building up your power.

When you add to memory, recall, the accomplishments made possible by exercising power over yourself, you are building self-esteem. This is covered in much more detail in later chapters where we will address how to exercise your power over yourself.

~~~

Self-confidence
17

"Everyone you meet is mainly worried about what you think of them."

One of the survival tricks your ancestors learned was how to deal with dominance and the unpleasant feeling of being judged. This was critical for survival as the strong leader was never going to allow another to take what he or she had acquired, usually by force. Within the tribe those that survived to breed are the ones who learned strategies for keeping the boss on side and convincing him or her that they were not a challenge.

In your mind, go back a few hundred generations. A strong and potentially lethal leader would pass silent judgement on all he or she encountered and if you were there, you would feel a tinge of fear each time you were assessed. Over time, you became part of the background and unless you did something unusual, you were not assessed very often. It is one of the reasons teenagers need to 'fit in' to be part of the crowd, conform to the current fashion or meme.

In society now, only a couple of hundred generations later, these instincts are still as strong as ever, as there has not been sufficient time for them to have dissolved despite no longer being essential for survival. It's a major contributor to our instinct to conform and to be so easily influenced by peer pressure. We need to belong or to live in fear.

Another far more dangerous act was walking alone into another tribe. The wrong move here was a guarantee of death. You might think about this the next time you walk into a room full of people. Your subconscious knows you are being assessed and not just by one potential threat. Your subconscious does not believe you are not in mortal danger.

Today this is not reality at all but the most extraordinary circumstances involving wild-eyed men with guns, but your subconscious is not taking any chances. How do you think your ancestors survived to breed you?

All is not lost however as it works in reverse too. When you walk into that room full of strangers, just about all of them feel pretty secure, mainly because 'safety in numbers' and they probably don't stand out from the crowd.

Despite this, every one of those people in the room has the slight instinctive fear of the 'doubtful' newcomer. What would raise their fear factor just a tad is concern you may single them out of the pack for attention, the action of a predator. Their subconscious doesn't know for absolute sure if the person that just walked into the room is a lethal danger or not, so that super-sensitive survival instinct holds them back just a little, in case you are bad news on legs.

This is an important point to keep in mind, **everyone you ever met has been mostly concerned about what YOU think of them, rather than assessing your social status.**

We should probably, for emphasis, repeat that. **Everyone *you meet is mainly worried about what you think of them.***

It may not seem that way because in the crowd they know they are safe but there is that underlying fear that you may spot their weaknesses and single them out. If they were made to look small, shameful, weak or any one of a dozen little fears they have locked up inside them, they know they would just 'die'.

Every one of these people has a survival instinct that tells them to be careful until you tell them, intentionally or otherwise, that they are equal to or more powerful than you. Until you do that, they will be respectful, just in case.

You notice I said they are all holding back a little in case you spot their weakness? This is a key piece of knowledge you need to manage any social situation and this is how you implement that knowledge.

The scan
Imagine for a moment someone is trying to guess if you are unsure of yourself, fearful, timid, blush easily,

stammer in front of an audience or any other fear that lurks inside your mind.

What happens in that critical first few seconds? If you suggest they take a good hard look at you, assessing you, looking at your dress sense, judging your appearance, you are right. That is exactly what they are doing. It has evolved into being a very quick act for two reasons.

If one party took too long, the other might assume they have been evaluated as a threat to be dealt with and decide to strike first. The very survival of your ancestors depended on making and passing this scrutiny countless times and each time it caused fear because of the potentially fatal consequences. You still have that reaction embedded deep in your coding and nothing you can ever do will remove it. Does that sound like bad news?

"Yes of course it is, how can I stop this from happening?" Well there is some good news. While you can't strip this piece of code from your DNA, the mind, like any other computer, has a hierarchy of coding and some pieces of code cannot be run simultaneously. They are, in a sense, incompatible.

Access Denied! — *The ability to assess others and the acceptance of being assessed cannot be processed at the same time. Your computer cannot process conflicting commands.*

The fear of being assessed can only be felt if your computer is in 'being assessed' mode. It cannot produce this fear if your brain is already using the scanner for assessing someone else. This might seem like a tie, a draw and that would not be so bad either but you can do better than that, you can win this tussle.

How do you know someone is assessing you? Well you can see they stop for a half-second or so and look at you, concentrating their full attention on you, totally oblivious to all else. It may be quick but it is powerful because your instincts kick in immediately and you feel fear or at least consternation. They feel the same because they know you are assessing them. For the moment, it ends in a draw but if you decide they've made a bad assessment of you, the fear lingers. No wonder you want to go home, to run away.

Now think. What must it feel like for the other person if you don't stop? You meet their gaze and hold it for two or three seconds, then draw it, like a fingernail on a blackboard, down to their neck or shoulders then scan back up to meet their gaze.

This entire one or two second event sets off alarm bells in their brain, raises their 'fight or flight' mechanism and generally puts their subconscious on red alert. This mismatch of assessment time has not only put them in a position of uncertainty, but you have denied your brain access to the 'being assessed' piece of code.

Until you show them you are unsure, their subconscious is urging them to be extremely cautious in case you are dangerous. It's not fear of a lethal attack, its fear of exposing the secret that you may have just discovered when you did the scan. They just don't know for 100% sure that you did not find it. For all they know, you may, as Douglas Adams wrote, have a brain bigger than a planet and can see all their fears. They just don't know until you tell them.

This is a good time to keep your mouth shut because you will never have this degree of dominance over them again. The more you talk, the more you reveal the more information they have, to assess you. The less you reveal the longer that first impression will be filed away in their subconscious 'just in case'.

Just as this applies to a single individual, it can apply to an entire room full of people. Obviously, you can't eyeball everyone at the same time but you can select the most likely person and importantly, deny your brain access to the 'being assessed' piece of coding. The more time you spend assessing members of the group, the longer you exclude your fear and demonstrate the confidence your performance suggests. Take your time, assess as many as you can. When combined with an upright stance, shoulders back, chin up and garnished with a slight smile, this is a killer entrance to any social situation. Just remember to keep your mouth shut.

Now we are equipped with the knowledge of how fear arises and the way to deny it access. With a little practice you can easily develop your confidence and I suggest a lot of practice. Every shop you enter, every group you encounter, practice your ability to control access to your 'being assessed' coding and a more confident life will emerge.

~~~

Armour
18

You can carry into social everts, something that is both armour and a weapon, silence. There's no need to be antisocial but silence is powerful. I don't mean 'shrinking-into-the-corner' or 'please don't-look-at-me' silence, I mean centre-stage 'bemused-confident' silence. Silence is the exercise of power, silence shows restraint, confidence. Laconic answers create uncertainty, stir slight hints of fear of what you might be thinking, passing judgement. It taps into deep seated fears.

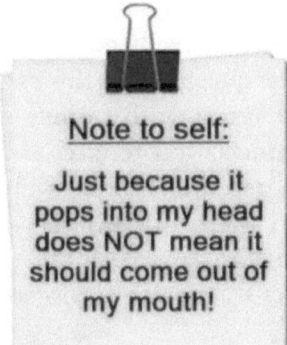

Note to self:

Just because it pops into my head does NOT mean it should come out of my mouth!

No matter how confident others may feel, the uncertainty of your silence can be unnerving. You could be preparing an attack; you could be thinking they are idiots (equally uncomfortable thoughts for them) you could be so far ahead of them they are inclined to spend some resources checking what they've revealed already. In that sense it acts as at least a deterrent. A wry smile with quietude is some powerful effect.

You tend to receive more respect when you are obviously capable of holding your own in the present company. Your silence is taken as holding back on your power so as not to inflict too much judgement upon them. Your reticence, your quiet confidence, increases pressure on them to perform with the obvious benefit of removing pressure on you.

When they don't know what you are thinking, people begin to worry about how you are evaluating them and their presentation, their countenance, their speech or their value. The more overt, the more voluble, the louder and dominating their performance, the more you can be assured they are mightily uncomfortable with being unable to categorize you.

There is no need to reply to every statement. Most statements do not require even your acknowledgement let alone validation no matter how much it may be desired. In fact, there is no compulsion to answer every question. There is no rule that says you can't avoid answering a question by asking one. A really confident person may even bluntly ignore the question but this can be interpreted as just plain cocky and rude. By asking a question that requires an explanation, you remove the need to perform, keeping things easy and smooth while putting all the pressure back on them. In this sense, silence or at least reticence is acting as armour.
When you do answer, because YOU choose to do so, you can be very economical.

Despite what you may feel, there is no law or coercion that can force you to answer a question if you choose not to answer. There is absolutely nothing anyone can do about that bemused smile on your face.

People make assumptions easily and by intimating you are holding back on comments, lets them assume you know more than you do. People love to make assumptions. They're driven to it.

Quite the opposite effect occurs with people who chatter. Chatter shows up as a lack of confidence, a vain attempt to cover up one's anxiety. **Essentially you should think of chatter as reaching out for reassurance and you don't want to be 'needy'.** The more you talk, the more you reveal and the more you are exposed to accurate judgment. This is not in your interests.

If you are relaxed in the present company, safe within yourself and sure you are on solid ground, by all means open up a little, but do not expose any more of your thoughts than what you need to achieve the goal, be that merely passing the time until you leave, making your speech or delivering the message. Whatever your goal, you get it done better with economical conversation.

~~~

Part Three

Friendship

The next part of living a sweet life is all about friendship and it's far more complicated than it seems. As a case study, in the middle, we will have a look at one of Albert's friends, who mastered the art. Of all the interlinked skills that influence the mastering of a sweet life, understanding friendship has to be at or near the top of the list.

~~~

Loneliness
19

"We are all alone together."

I can only recall once feeling loneliness. It was my 21st birthday. I had moved back to my old hometown just a few days before and I'd lost touch with the few people I still knew.

Looking back, it seems I must have known instinctively what to do. Over the next few days, I simply acted as a friend to a couple of young guys I met casually, probably at a pub and it was business as usual.

This should not be taken to trivialize the depressing situation when one suffers from chronic loneliness, often as a consequence of being unable to connect with others on anything more than a superficial level.

When you feel you have no 'best friend' it can be frustrating and it certainly undermines your self-confidence, wondering what is wrong with you. Others have best friends, why don't I?

Often this is made worse when you are in company but feel like you are just taking up space, that no one is interested in you or in what you have to say. This can result in a feeling of complete isolation, even on a bus or train or walking around the shops, no one talks to you, no one is interested in you. Negative feelings and self-doubt thrive in these situations and we need to address the problem.

Well-intentioned but wrong is the advice handed out by parents and others "go out and make some friends" "join a club and make some friends". This is setting the unfortunate lonely individual up for failure. It suggests that it is possible to manufacture friends, to slap together a bunch of people that will not only like you but invite you for lunch and all their social occasions.

The inference is that one already knows how to have friends and it's just a matter of doing 'make friends' actions and all will be well. It also suggests that the individual is equipped to handle the stress that 'making friends' entails especially if one is not 'a natural'.

What parents usually fail to tell them is exactly how to do it, probably because they have never stopped to consider how they managed to come by their own friends. The important thing to know about this is that it is not possible to simply 'make' a friend. One simply cannot force another to befriend you.

Becoming
If the well-intentioned advice was 'go out and be a friend', the success rate would go up dramatically because this is precisely what you need to do. Most of us

make friends without knowing or even being aware of the process. Once you stop and consider how it happens, it makes it a whole lot easier to replicate the circumstances and make as many friends as you want.

Despite what I said earlier that you can't make friends, this applies in the literal sense of manufacturing them. You can in fact make friends by default with a simple action: become one.

Although at first this sounds overly simplistic, this is the way to acquire all the friends you will ever desire. If you act as a friend, go through the actions of a person who is already a friend, the person on the receiving end will start to perceive you as 'a friend'. Repeat.

The actions of a friend are what? A friend will be pleased to see you, greet you with enthusiasm and you don't even have to bark, jump onto their lap or wag your tail. Fortunately.

When I greet my friends, I leave no doubt I am pleased to see them again. It is always with enthusiasm and a laugh. People like to be around happy people, especially happy people who like them. It makes you feel good too.

People expect a friend will have something good to say to them, to ask about them and their interests, to extend an invitation, offer to help. If you do any of these things, they will recognize them as the actions of a friend, whether you are currently a friend or not, with or without a tail.
Yes, they may be surprised, but they will also be pleased, not least because you didn't try to lick their face. No

wonder they are pleased to hear from you. Most people are not particularly good at making friends so this puts you at a considerable advantage.

Even though you could address this like any other task and set out goals, timelines and actions, each of us is presented with a lot of opportunities, most of which we ignore. If your current circle is really small and you don't get out much but you are still prepared to give it a go, then yes, you should consider making some effort to put some discipline into it.

Best friend
What someone who is lonely might desire more than anything else is a 'confidant' a true, best friend. A 'confidant' is someone with whom you feel secure sharing some private thoughts that you would not like shared with others. Usually this will be someone very close, emotionally and/or physically intimate. A word of warning here about a little quirk of human nature; the psychological effect upon us when we get into close proximity with another, like a hairdresser or masseuse for example.

This mimics our closeness with very good friends, intimate friends and can provoke us to impart information that really should be kept to ourselves. Hairdressers have a reputation for being on the receiving end of some pretty intimate conversations, not without reason. Just be mindful next time you let someone touch your hair.

The Mechanics of it
20

A good way to start building your friend bank is thinking about people you know from your neighbourhood, work and any associations you belong to. You might broaden this list to include people you interact with incidentally, service people, shop people, tradesmen, delivery people, just about anyone you will meet again. Whichever way you get to be in contact, what is important to recognize is that it does not matter if your first impression of these people is that they are not likely prospects for future friends, only that you may see them again.

The most important thing you can do in this moment is remember their name. The best way to do that is ask, then repeat it, check that you have pronounced it correctly, ask for the spelling if it is not common, mention if you know someone with the same name or if you don't know anyone with the same name, tell them you like the name, but whatever you do, make a fuss about their name. The more you talk about their name the better you will remember it and this is critical.

At the first private moment, write it down. You will not remember it otherwise, no matter how highly you regard your memory. The dullest pencil beats the sharpest memory every time.

Upon meeting them again, nothing makes an impression on a casual acquaintance so much as remembering their name. It tells them they are special to you, that you care enough to remember them. You are more than halfway to making a new friend with that one small effort.

Even the lowliest most humble person can turn out to be someone special, a treasure. It does happen, albeit not every time. There are lots of easy reasons to by-pass someone. Maybe they are boring, not my type of person, too smart, too dumb, too old, too young. Yes there are lots of reasons but that is a serious mistake.

Winning the lottery is not the object of the exercise. In any case, are you so special that you don't have time for anyone that does not immediately present as someone who is not useful to you?

It is true that in some cases an act of friendship will be met with some suspicion, especially between the sexes, but that does not cost you anything and after the recipient gets a similar greeting next time, your position as a casual friend will gradually become reality.
The more of these casual friends you acquire, the more close friends that evolve from the group and this is the purpose of the exercise. Just remember that these are just new friends and you have absolutely no right to

expect anything from them in return. You are offering to be a friend and that is all.

It takes a certain amount of work to act as a friend. Overcoming the lack of interest we often have in other people, takes a conscious effort. Often a person who seems an unlikely or uninteresting friend, turns out to be very amenable and if you are mercenary about it, useful. If you have few friends, it is not important or wise even, to be choosy about who your new friends are going to be. It is a lot easier to de-select friends, than it is to make new ones, so in the beginning, you need to put together a large number of potential friends.

Secrets
When you do build up your network of friends, one thing that may crop up that sounds like great progress but comes with a caution.

There are a few questions that pique one's interest more than "can I tell you a secret?". Perhaps only "I have a confession" is more intriguing but beware. Once you accept the information, you may feel the weight of responsibility for the consequences of keeping it secret and that may not be easy or comfortable. Essentially it now becomes your secret, your burden too in some cases. Sure, you feel a positive vibe, clearly the other person holds you in some regard, but there is always a cost. It's not something you should go into lightly, not that you necessarily get much warning of what their deep and dark secret is beforehand.

Initial contact
You already know a lot of your future friends. You have met them or at least nodded to them in passing. Those who are good at making friends seem to automatically do two things, keep it simply friendly and brief. By brief, I mean from 10 to 60 seconds. It's essentially a 'hello' followed by a question. The question will vary with circumstances but one that relates to an existing or immediate past event is best.

An example is if you saw a neighbour have a bit of trouble with his/her rubbish bin or a power black-out or a storm, anything really, all you need do is ask if they were affected by the event. Keep it very friendly, brief and finish with "just thought I'd check if everything is ok" or you might say "if you ever need a hand to….". That is all that is required of an initial contact.

Do not go out of your way to approach them unnecessarily and preferably not for at least a week or two, at which point you may have thought up an invitation that is easy for them to decline. The invitation could be something as simple as saying "I'm going to the markets tomorrow. If you need anything or wanted to come, I'm going about 10 o'clock". No more than that. Be brief and be gone. It's important they understand that you care, but don't care too much.

Subsequent contacts can be a bit longer, although you are always in a bit of a rush so they know you are not going to demand much of their personal time or space.

Once you have got yourselves on friendly talking terms, just put them on the regular contact list and occasionally make an offer of something free. Produce like eggs or vegetables are a wonderful gift that almost guarantees a friendship. All gifts, even the lowly, least valuable, come with a highly valuable box or wrapper called 'friendship'. Most people feel they don't have enough of it.

If things progress past this point and you like it, by all means get closer but if they are not likely close future friends, don't take them off the regular contact list. Always maintain your investment in people. One day it may pay, but even if it doesn't, investment is a numbers game and the more you have, the better you get at making them..

If you are driving near a casual friend's home, you could stop for what is essentially a social call but one that does not demand a long conversation or coffee or an invitation to stay. To be effective this can be as little as pulling into the driveway and saying that you are just passing and thought you'd say "hello" and or ask about a previous event.

If they seem receptive and invite you in, by all means accept but don't take advantage. Stay for a little and leave. You have achieved your goal, improved their day, made them feel valued and that is all the motive you need. Do not do this in expectation of receiving a reward. Do not be an exploiter. Do not expect your friends to do anything or share anything and you will not be disappointed.

~~~

Selfish Friendship
21

"Friends are the family you get to choose."

We want to believe that friendship is a relationship that develops over time and eventually each would come to stand by the other in equal measure. A friend is someone who is 'there for you', cares about you and is always willing to help you, right? A friend will laugh with you in good times, sit with you through bad times and tell you when you are wrong. What's not to like? In an ideal world, you would have lots of friends and all would be just like that.

At its core, friendship is essentially a desire to receive benefits in the form of companionship, physical assistance, shared outings, entertainment and many other things. We want friends so we can enjoy being 'in the gang' and we need them so we don't feel isolated and vulnerable, however it's important to come to terms with the idea that you really want friends for purely selfish reasons, to further your life and comfort.

Once you accept that, it is easier to accept that everyone else feels the same way and you can let go of the unrealistic idea that friendship is the desire to be close to you, to revel in your company. No one is your friend for your benefit alone. When the friendship is no longer useful to others, it will go into torpor, a steady state that can be revived once your company provides a renewal of benefit for them.

Marcus Aurelius, the educated Stoic philosopher and last Roman Emperor of the Pax (peaceful) era wrote:

Whenever a person's lack of shame (or substitute the thoughtless act of a friend) *offends you, you should immediately ask yourself, "Is it possible for there to be no shameless people in the world?" It isn't, and you should therefore stop demanding the impossible. He's just one of those shameless people who must necessarily exist in the world.*

He points out that our anger is a failure not of the other but a failure in our perception.

You'll find that none of the people who make you lose your temper has done anything that might affect your mind for the worse; and outside of the mind there's nothing that is truly detrimental or harmful for you... After all, you even had the resources, in the form of your ability to think rationally, to appreciate that he was likely to commit that fault, yet you forgot it and are now surprised that he did exactly that.

We know, or at least if we are adults we should know, that we cannot change others, that we can only change ourselves, so the solution is rather simple, we need to classify our friends, peer down the microscope upon their personality and give them a fancy Latin name. Or not.

Robin Dunbar is a British anthropologist, evolutionary psychologist and a specialist in primate behaviour. He is one of the very few people who has a number named after him. He is best known for formulating Dunbar's number, a measurement of the 'cognitive limit to the number of individuals with whom any one person can maintain stable relationships'.

Dunbar's number is often quoted as 150 but in fact the number he made famous is 148 and it has been rounded out. Further, 150 itself is just the upper limit of four approximate numbers being, 5,15,50 and 150. What you might notice about these is that each number is approximately 3 times larger than the preceding number.

The number 5 is the core group, the second group, close relationships has 15 people, (three times as many). The next circle is 50 people, moderately well-known on at least nodding/greeting terms and finally, social, up to 150 members approximately, typical size of a small village.

While Dunbar's number may be mildly interesting, the information itself has little impact on improving our lives. Despite reading much on the subject and paying deference to the very smart people who figure out and write about these matters, the psychologists, evolutionary anthropologists and experts in general, they appear to ignore or perhaps dismiss what to me is an important distinction.

It's all well and good to label the 5 or so people in your inner circle as the core group and the next 15 as close friends but what is the point if you don't recognize that some members of these groups may not be prepared to do much to help if you need it?

Dunbar's number infers that the 15 close friends are the ones you can depend on and if you can't by definition, they are not in the 15. I do not accept this delineation.

I've noted many times, after assessing my friendships for more than 50 years, that some of my closest friends, ones I spend time with on a regular basis, friends with whom I share a meal and long in-depth conversations over many years, are so self-centric they wouldn't give a blind duck a push into a pond.

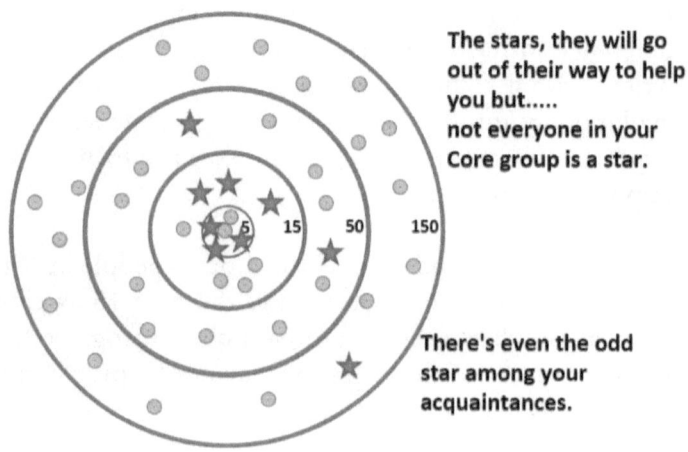

Within your orbit, think of your friends as many planets and a few stars. Some are willing to take actions to help me and some are not. This does not mean I can't enjoy the company of the recalcitrants. It does not mean they don't invite me to share their company, their activities and sometimes, their good fortune.

The reason they do that, is not because they are concerned about my welfare or happiness, it's because it is difficult to enjoy one's good fortune if there is no one to share it with.

In other words, they share with me, improving my life **largely in their own interests**, pursuing their happiness in a way that is perfectly natural and effective. They can and should improve their life this way and we should too.

~~~

To Friends Of Friends
22

"An OF friend will lend you his truck. A To friend will help you load the body."

It sounds like a no-neck heavyweight making a toast at a mafia wake, 'to friends of friends' but I'm afraid it's nothing so menacing, or interesting for that matter. Punctuation matters and we will see why shortly.

Most friendship pain comes from the collision between our expectations of our friends and their needs, to which they naturally, like us, give their full attention. It's a collision between our expectations and reality.

The amount of angst we feel is up to us. It can be a very painful experience, relived many times as we indignantly review and replay the slight, the insult that caused our grief. It can also be ignored and forgotten, easier to do when you expect them to do what they do.
When you have a low expectation level, the collision is avoided altogether and the result is a no-pain relationship, where one is free to enjoy all the best the friendship offers and none of the disappointment.

We need to hold that thought close by, when friends are off-handed, thoughtless or seemingly indifferent to our immediate situation. Don't get me wrong, I'm not a 'turn the other cheek' kind of guy, but if you know or feel confident that a friend is not the kind that naturally looks to help others, why feel angry when they do what comes naturally. (That's a rhetorical question if you're wondering why there's no question mark.)

Friends come in two versions, not, as one would expect, 'close' and 'others' or 'friends' and 'acquaintances'. The two groups we need to consider are the TO and the OF friends.

The most important thing is knowing, if someone from your 'Close' friends group, is, by nature, a TO or an OF friend.

For most of us, our friends list runs about 90% OF friends, that is a list of people you are friendly with but who would not go out of their way to help you. The other 10% are probably TO friends, that is people you are friendly with who would help you if you needed it, even if it were inconvenient for them. In other words, they are a friend *to* you.

Once you start looking at your friends as being either TO or OF you stop having expectations and avoid disappointment by expecting OF friends to do anything for your benefit.

Before you rush off labelling your friends, be aware that we are dealing with humans who are at best a contrary and unpredictable species. Some of your friends you label as TO friends, those will do anything for you, will go a certain distance but no more, they may be on the TO side but have some OF in them as well.

Some are prepared to go the whole hog, others not so much, so even if you do consider someone a TO or true friend, be aware there will probably be a limit and it might be lower than you think.

On the upside, there are people you barely know who just want to be good people and will go out of their way to help you, far more than some in the 'Core' and Good-friends groups. Don't be too stressed if you discover you don't have many genuine TO friends. Most people don't but are deluded, thinking they have a lot more than they do, right up to the point where they need them and that's when the emotions take a hit.

If you are practical, you accept that your friends will only go so far and most importantly realize, **you cannot do anything about it**. You can't manufacture friends who will do anything for you and you can't get them from loyalty. At best you might guilt-trip someone you've suffered for.

Trying to upgrade your friends into the small TO (true) friends group will depend largely on that person's character, rather more than anything you can do, past making the effort of being a TO friend to them.

Don't worry if nearly all your friends are OF friends. There is nothing wrong with having a lot of OF friends. They can be entertaining and helpful to you, so long as they don't have to sacrifice anything much for your benefit.

~~~

Listening
23

Albert was telling me the other day about his old friend Big Ronnie, who was a special people person, an expert in friendship. This seems an appropriate place to mention his gift. This is what Albert told me.

Meet Big Ronnie

"After all the rain over the last few days, it was another beautiful Sunday morning at Bunnings. Transplant Kenny was on the boom gate, as usual and once we got past the exhaust fumes coming from the little men in the big American 4wd trucks, looking smug and clutching their handbag of goodies and their new man-sized nail guns, the air inside the trade doors was crisp and refreshing.

I was somewhat alarmed at first, but the American girl screaming over the loudspeaker turned out to be a famous singer. It was good when she stopped. The latest music tunes apparently, but I don't think it will take.

It reminded me of a morning some years ago when we'd brought our daughter Offin Faithful and her new calf with us. We got the calf after Daisy, our house cow, died. We buried her at a special place on our property at Titsupp Downs. (Not Offin, the cow.)

Actually we got Offin two calves to start with but we had to give one away. Offin is not good at keeping her calves together her mother said. But the one we kept, well Offin really loved it and it was lucky we had the 1973 Leyland P76 with the cavernous boot because her calf got so big, its head would stick out one back window and its tail the other side.

Cows produce four things really well, meat, milk, methane and fertilizer. We were ok with that, mostly, as the windows were down anyway but cleaning out the really wet bits that got down between the glass and the door, not so much and the manager complained about the smell in aisle 47 in the trade drive in, so we were thinking maybe next time we might leave her at home. And the calf of course.

After all, Offin never made any mess in aisle 47. Well, there was that one time but she was younger then. I only mention this because once inside, I saw the back of a wet sweaty xxxxl hiviz shirt with a sparsely ginger top, blocking aisle 19, getting directions from Old Diamond, the beam of heavenly light from the massed fluos reflecting off his head. (Old Diamond's, not ginger nut's.) It reminded me of my long-passed mate Big Ronnie.

Big Ronnie was a butcher and every afternoon after working at the shop, he and his boss Ralph Saveloy, would head across the road to the Noe Alms Hotel for a few drinks. It wasn't always easy either. If the barmaid called in sick, you'd have to pour your own, for obvious reasons.
Even Tall Terry Tucker's mate Toad the truck driver, would have to take a turn behind the bar and he was certainly well armed. With tattoos too.

Now Big Ronnie was big, which is funny about nick names, because Tall Terry is not and Bluey has red hair and Skinny is, well ok some nick names are the opposite. Big Ronnie did not look like a ladies man but they loved him. The funeral was packed with women, most of whom considered themselves 'close' and strangely there was little animosity. It seems they would forgive Big Ronnie anything and one day, Ralph Saveloy told me Big Ronnie's secret with women. I hardly dare tell you.

It seems that Big Ronnie loved just two things, beer and people, in particular the non-male variety.

By 8pm at the Noe Alms Hotel, Big Ronnie would decide he'd had enough and go home for a steak. He was a butcher after all, and knock off a carton of beer for a nightcap.

But it's what he did with women that was so amazing. He was one of a rare breed indeed. It's a well-established fact that almost no man can listen to a woman and not offer his manly advice. So extraordinary a skill had Big Ronnie, that he was once featured on David

Attenborough's 'Rare and Endangered Species' program.

He was beyond doubt, an accomplished listener, a master, a craftsman. He could listen all night without raising a sweat, exhausting even women who had several days-worth of unspoken words left over. He'd listen to every word, never once suggesting a course of action, never once giving a word of manly advice and they would enthusiastically take him to their bosom. And quite a few other parts too, apparently.

Big Ronnie used to visit me and Neerlee at Titsupp Downs every now and then, to do a taste test of my latest brew. It was a Saturday afternoon in Autumn, that fateful day after we had tested about a dozen large bottles, when, through the slightly open door we saw my wonderful wife Neerlee Faithful and my daughter Offin as they were leading Daisy, our then house cow to the barn for milking. Tall Terry was probably out driving his truck.

I should say at this point that ever since I've known her, Neerlee has had the need for XXL blouses, a trait that she has passed on to our daughter Offin Faithful and to her sister Canbie who lives in Nudgee. Their unusually modest waist size tends to attract some attention too, although I don't know why people are interested in their waist sizes.

When we go to Bunnings, people stare especially at Offin. I think it might be because Offin is famous for being very handy with an axe and has won a lot of medals. Some say you can hear her ring bark for miles.

In an uncharacteristically careless moment, Big Ronnie commented on Daisy's swollen teats at milking time and the company she was in. Well, we laughed and laughed. We opened another bottle and laughed some more. That evening, my son-in-law Tall Terry who isn't, Offin Faithful's husband, joined us for dinner. I couldn't let the chance go by, so I had to relate the funny story I had shared with Big Ronnie.

Well, Tall Terry and I laughed and we laughed. We laughed some more. Then I remember it was quiet for a little while.

I must say the nurses were good though, polite, caring, very understanding. They smiled a lot when I explained what had happened, probably to give me some encouragement. Probably helps with the healing process too. When I got home a few days later, we didn't talk about Daisy.

In fact, I don't think her name ever came up again before she passed and I know for sure I won't be telling that story again. Any funny stories actually.

Now, the calf has grown and taken on Daisy's job. Offin and Tall Terry still come over now and again for dinner and I can walk without wincing now, so all is good. I miss Big Ronnie though."
Well, that's what Albert told me anyway.

~~~

On Being 'To'
24

Once you have considered your friends and can see them in their true light, you should think about being a friend. To many people, you are just an OF friend, because they don't think you would go out of your way to help them.

The depth of the TO friendship you have with others is determined by how much inconvenience you find acceptable. For someone you care about deeply, that could be a lot.

When you take stock, think about how people would rate you. If you feel that most of the people you know, would never rely on you to help them, you may draw an unpleasant conclusion, one that may include words we don't use in polite company, but I'm sure you're not like that.

Pareto's Principle
Our lives are governed to a large extent by broad 'rules' that we find to be generally true. One such 'law' or 'rule' is named after an Italian economist Vilfredo Pareto who

noted in 1896 that 80% of land in Italy was owned by 20% of the people and this led to his realization that these proportions apply to many other fields.

Simply stated, for many outcomes, roughly 80% of consequences come from 20% of causes. The 80% majority of accidents come from 20% of the hazards, 80% of crime is committed by 20% of criminals, even computer code faults are 80/20. Microsoft noted that 80% of code bugs could be fixed in 20% of the lines and users only access 20% of Word functions 80% of the time.

You will find this 'rule' appears frequently in other parts of your life, 20% of customers are responsible for 80% of complaints, 20% of buyers account for 80% of sales, 20% of neighbours make 80% of the nuisance noise and even here, talking about friendships.

If you have a lot of friends, based on the 80/20 rule, the more OF friends you have, the more TO friends you will acquire. To get and keep these TO friends you must at the very least be a TO friend to the few you have.

You can't manufacture these but it is a numbers game. Over time you can allocate all your friends to the appropriate category and most will end up in the OF department, where you enjoy their company but expect little more than a warm welcome. Another reason to acquire a large number of OF friends is that sometimes someone you least suspected would be a good TO friend, turns out to be a wonderful asset that you would not have recognized from a casual or passing acquaintance.

The benefits of friendship are many, from great conversations, invites to social affairs (if you like that sort of thing) help with home projects, expansion of your circle of friends, invites to join associations, invites for fishing trips, boating holidays, long lunches and sharing hobbies among many others.

From a business perspective, friendships can produce some good contacts, increased business opportunities and investment help. The bottom line is, provided it is not taken to the extreme, the expression 'more is better' is true.

Investment
Friendships, whether we like to think of them this way or not, are an investment and a very practical one at that, providing benefits at least as good as many financial investments and in many cases, a great deal more. Friendships don't require capital to invest, just some time and effort and they can deliver great rewards.

Your friends-portfolio needs to be tendered like a caring and keen gardener looks after his or her garden. You should call your friends at least once a month. All of them. It's almost certain that they will not call you because they are unlikely to consciously think about the value of your friendship until they need you. Are you offended they haven't called? Would you be offended if your stockbroker did not call you once a month to tell you how well your share portfolio is doing?
As your friends-portfolio is an investment program, you need to monitor and tend to it like any other. The return on your investments is uncertain but if you put in the

time to monitor them, choose wisely and have a wide spread of different types of investment, you will succeed. Sound familiar? This is the advice you will receive from any competent financial adviser.

How soon do you expect a return on your investments? Of course, it depends on luck, circumstances, maybe the economy, many things. You would be naïve to believe you will get a great return on every investment and next week too. That is ridiculous. Each person you befriend, each one you help and support is a potential helper to you, often when you least expect it.

My friends are an endless source of joy, not just their company, but also their willingness to share their good fortune with me, someone who appreciates the hard work they put in to achieve their goals. They appreciate that I appreciate the difficulties they faced, the trials and tribulations they endured to arrive at their success. A friend understands and embraces their journey. If I was not prepared to be a friend, I would have no friend. It really is that simple.

Extreme friends
It may sound incredible, but you can be friends with those at the very edges of friendship and few are closer to the edge than the hyper-critical narcissist.

The hyper-critical narcissist is someone who criticizes everything and everyone. They criticize how you drive to how you dress to how you perform almost any task. Very little data, often just one sample, is required to make these determinations. Every problem that needs solving must be solved their way.

They hate being delayed for even a few seconds. When they decide it's time to go, it must be this instant. Their ability to function in relationships is limited with little regard for the feelings, plans or interests of others. They talk about themselves and their current interests almost exclusively. They're often boastful and monopolize conversations. They look down on most people as they perceive almost everyone as inferior.

What, you may ask, could one possibly gain by being friends with someone with these shortcomings? The hyper-critical narcissist is not spoiled for choice in friends so they will welcome the attention, which they will interpret as admiration. They can be extreme in other ways too, often highly intelligent and capable of scintillating conversation dealing with many fascinating subjects, which they will dominate of course.

They can also be entertaining and generous, possibly an attempt to help them be accepted by others. Provided you are aware of the limitations of engagement with them, keeping your expectations low and prepared to not have your opinions or interests considered, short engagements can be a reasonably pleasant, even amusing experience. An ability to grit your teeth and bite your tongue may be an advantage and good practice for you.

Exploitive friends
There are people who already understand how friendship works and are prepared to use it to exploit. You need to be aware that some of your OF friends will be capable and ready to exploit your friendship, using you only to further their agenda and unwilling to do

anything for you in return. As soon as the benefits you provide dry up, you will be dumped.

This is absolutely no reason to snub their friendship and not as bad as it sounds, if you have judiciously assessed what type of friend they are. If you are fully aware that they are mere OF friends that provide you with entertainment or other benefits but you are sure they don't give a damn about you personally, you expect them to dump you.

In any case, we know we get a benefit from helping others so even when exploited to some extent, we still get something of a win. You may not hold them in high regard and if you are smart and have many OF friends and hopefully a couple of TO friends, you will not miss the exploiter.

Then there is the added benefit, if at some point in the future, they now find a need of your friendship, you can, with a kindly smile, extract a price commensurate with their treachery.

~~~

Must Do List
25

There are a few things you should have in mind as 'must do' things, to or for your friends. This list is much shorter than things you should never do, but consider these the positive actions of a friend. They will stand you in good stead and improve your welcome immensely.

Some people, for whatever strange reason, seem to be reluctant to acknowledge the achievements of others. For example, a man can show his friend the new gismo or construction he built, a new patio added to the house, the latest project and is justly or otherwise proud of what he has done. Many friends and acquaintances will grudgingly nod or make some small criticism but under no circumstances voice any praise whatsoever.

All you need do is make some fuss about that person's legitimate right to some praise and acknowledgement. Sometimes it may take a little effort to find the praiseworthy parts, but don't be stingy. Afterall, it costs nothing. People like to hear this in a one-to-one conversation, but they LOVE to hear this in a social situation.

Social situations offer the most powerful opportunities. Find something, anything, praise-worthy about your friend. Abilities, achievements, natural assets, clever solutions, there are many possibilities. Find one or more and repeat them in every social setting. You will have at least one more OF friend who always wants you to be there when people are gathered.

Look especially for those situations where your OF friend is in the company of his or her friends or family. Never miss the chance to tell everyone or comment about their success. Compliment their achievements, their knowledge, experience, attitude, driving, whatever, it's what friends do.

Another subject that brings him/her joy is when you happen to share your friend's opinion and make it known in company. Nothing is more joyous and interesting to your friend than hearing his or her opinion come from you. If you feel you don't agree, best temper your opinion to maintain the friendship.

Maybe not something you must do, but should sometimes, ask for a small favour, to borrow (item returned promptly) or just ask for an opinion.

When people do something for you, they feel good and if you show you appreciate their effort, you go a long way to cementing a friendship. (The pedant in me recoils from the term 'cementing' in the full knowledge that cement is only one component in concrete, which is what we mean when 'cementing' a relationship, but 'concreting' just doesn't sound right.)

Greasing the wheels
Lies are generally considered to be a bad thing, but in reality, we couldn't live in a society where everyone told the truth, the absolute truth and nothing but the truth. Our social cohesion depends on being conservative in our critique and economical with the truth. If your favourite aunt, the one who named you in her will, gifted you a book of poems she wrote, how do you respond, with your heartfelt opinion a full-on critique of her work or perhaps a more gentile response regardless of your opinion?

We prefer little 'white' lies especially if it means others don't have to make tough decisions, like taking you out of a will.

~~~

Definitely Don't
26

"Don't let your friend take a laxative and a sleeping pill together."

It will probably come as no surprise, the list of things you should not do to your friends is considerably longer than the ones you should make an effort to do. Top of the list and one of the most common friendship destroyers is borrowing money.

Borrow money
There are few things you can do worse than ask your friends to lend you money. You put them in an invidious position where they feel they have little choice and this guarantees resentment. In addition, if you need to borrow money, it is almost certain you are not in control of your finances and there is a very high probability that you cannot pay it back quickly and in one lump sum. Even if you do, the repayment transaction is uncomfortable for both parties.

If you are tempted to ask for financial help from your friends, DON'T.

Happiness comes from having all the components under control and while they are all important, having surplus money, is possibly the most important. If you have to ask your friends for money, you are clearly not financially secure. You need to take immediate and drastic action to utterly change the way you are doing things. Fortunately, the way to do this will be revealed in great detail in the following chapters.

Advice
If Big Ronnie hadn't been a butcher,, he would have been a scientist, although I might have made that up. Anyway, the story goes that Big Ronnie used to say that the most plentiful element in the universe after hydrogen is unsolicited advice. It is of so little value, nobody wants it.

Aren't we all tempted to give voice, not only to our opinion but offer advice too, whether our victim wants it or not? No matter how tempting, how much you think your friend will benefit from your wisdom, don't.

Braggers
Friends don't big-note themselves, brag of their achievements. If someone lets you rave on about your achievements and moments of glory, it is because **they** are good at friendship and you are not. Keep it up and eventually they too will tire of your company. You are literally a pain and merely tolerated. You don't want to be that.

Story toppers
One of the most irritating and often ridiculed habits is that of the story topper. Someone relates a tale of some

amusement or adventure and the story topper just has to come up with a better story of what happened to them. Worse than bragging, most people think the story topper is lying or at least exaggerating, so not only does the story topper fail in his bid to be admired, but the childish action also brought them down in the estimation of all present.

Forcing opinions
Friends do not force their opinions on others. In the next chapter we look at the way we form our opinions and realize why some hold their opinions like their life depended on it, convinced, without a shadow of doubt, their opinion is correct.

There is little point in trying to persuade them otherwise and zero benefit to you in antagonizing them. We intuitively think that everyone forms their opinions the same way we do, but reality is different.

You can indulge a pleasure in some cases of discussing subjects upon which you have utterly diverse views but for the sake of your wider circle of friends and the extraordinary benefits that flow from having lots of friends, it is not worth attempting to prove that your view is superior. In any case, it may not be so.

Conspiracy theories
One of the real friendship killers is the conspiracy theory, where the holder of the theory is keen to share the 'special' knowledge they have. There are literally tens of thousands of conspiracy theories and it is possible one of them is true but if you subscribe to unsubstantiated concepts, you should do two things.

First, consider that the idea is appealing because you would like it to be true. Second, recognize that the concept was presented to you before you already had an opinion on the subject so this is the first possibility and not necessarily the only possibility. Worse, this is not even your opinion it's one you borrowed from someone you don't even know because you haven't the knowledge, skill or perseverance to make your own.

Even if you are convinced, **do not** share this with your friends. You will only do yourself harm. Conspiracy theories lower you in the eyes of others and make most of us frustrated and irritated. Leave them behind or at the very least, leave them unspoken.

Your story
Friendships develop from two people revealing something of themselves, essentially exposing a vulnerability. This works by taking it in turns to reveal small parts of your past. Naturally we prefer to talk about the better parts of our story, the less ignoble parts, not so much.

This act of sharing needs to be treated carefully and it is best if we can get a balanced outcome, where each party shows the other a little of themselves but not too much. Too much is more often the result of added alcohol.

We are interested in our stories. It's only natural and to some extent, necessary for establishing friendships but curbing it, keeping it in check is one of the hardest desires to control.

When someone shares part of their life experience with you, it is obvious you must listen and not just passively, listen and engage. Now it is your turn. You no doubt have a story to tell that could easily be linked to theirs but how far do you take it?

Think of the last conversation you had with a friend and ask yourself, how much time did we spend talking about what they were doing, his or her plans, work or play, activities and recent wins. If more than half was about them, you won. You are a great friend.

When we talk about ourselves endlessly, what we are saying is that our universe is so small, so bland, so stunningly uninteresting that we, at the centre of it, are the most interesting thing in our universe and that's all we want to talk about. That's sad.

If you suspect that sometimes you are a bit of a conversation hog (loquacious for those logophiles out there) and most of us, men especially, have been guilty of this occasionally (heavy sarcasm here) try to recall the word 'laconic'. Can you imagine Clint Eastwood, laconic in the flesh, chatting on relentlessly about himself? Me neither. Don't overdo it, curb yourself with a dose of Dirty Harry.

~~~

Understanding Your Friends
27

"We make the assumption that everyone sees life the way we do". – Miguel Angel Ruiz

It is not necessary to always keep your opinions to yourself, even though promoting yours at the expense of others will render null your efforts to build up a beneficial network.

In my imagination, I see Albert as one of those gentle folk who never impose their opinions upon others, possibly to compensate for my own indiscretions in this field.

It makes it easier to resist tearing into someone who has a contrary opinion to you, if you understand a couple of basic points.

Everyone has an opinion on big boxes, notable among them, politics and religion. Inside these boxes, there are slightly smaller boxes, like immigration, racism, inequality, minority rights and dozens of others. Each of these boxes contain many more, smaller boxes and you will probably agree with your friends about the general thrust of these, but inside them, there are many even smaller boxes and you will agree and disagree on the general thrust of those.

So it goes on. The point here is that it is pointless to discuss the big boxes because they contain too many boxes on which you both agree and disagree. Once you show yourself to disagree with your friend, you lay the ground for disaffection. In most cases, the friction caused by conflicting opinions can mostly be avoided by steering clear or at least brushing lightly past, discussions of the big boxes.

Couplers and De-couplers

We are mainly either a coupler, a 'contextualizer' if there were such a word, someone who puts every nuance of a subject into the assessment or a de-coupler. It is important to understand which of these you are and which of your friends is of the other variety.

A de-coupler is one who looks at things just in its own little box, ignoring the 'mother' box that it comes in and the box the mother box came in and all the other connected and associated boxes.

For example, a de-coupler could easily discuss the science and evidence for say, breeding humans to run faster, acknowledging that it could be done without supporting the idea that it should be done.

A 'coupler' or 'contextualizer' on the other hand, could be angry at this discussion because the idea is associated with racism and subjugation and you can't even discuss the concept of people breeding without assuming those discussing it are in favour of its implementation.

Richard Dawkins the famous biologist, documentary maker and renowned atheist, said on Twitter recently *"It's one thing to deplore eugenics (breeding humans) on ideological, political, moral grounds, it's quite another to conclude that it wouldn't work in practice."*

This made a lot of people angry even though what he said is fairly obvious, that if you bred humans for some trait then it would probably make that trait more common. He was quite explicit in saying he wasn't saying it was morally acceptable. Many people who read this took an altogether different meaning, that he was literally in favour of eugenics.

He had to go back on Twitter and make it clear (unsuccessfully as it happens) that no, he was not: *"I deplore the idea of a eugenic policy [but just] as we breed cows to yield more milk, we could breed humans to run faster or jump higher. Heaven forbid that we do it."*

The point of this anecdote it to highlight the differences in the way that people think. We are not all the same.

Another example could be an actor who is later found to be a miscreant or sexual predator but whose work showed them to be a brilliant actor. A de-coupler will put them in different boxes and acknowledge the brilliance of the acting while reviling the actions of the person. A contextualizer will refuse to even consider watching the film because the work and the person are as one. The contextualizer puts the entire picture into context and will never consider them separately.

You can see how easy it is for people to get into arguments when they basically agree on the one point but one separates the events and the other puts them together. Journalists, politicians and PR people who rely on ambiguous meanings, associations, implications and allusions to evoke feelings, impressions and ideas in their audience use the tools of context in their work.

The contextualizer looks at the de-coupler mystified, concluding they lack empathy while the de-coupler is equally mystified by what appears to be bias and the inability to think logically.

If at least we know that not everyone thinks in the same way, we can more easily hold back on our opinions and not harm our friendships with arguments that are fruitless, never to be settled or agreed upon because we look at each subject from a totally different but equally legitimate perspective.

Assumption

As if these totally opposed ways of thinking were not enough, we have also to contend with assumption. Our understanding of each other, our communication has a few obstacles strewn across the path, not only in terms of how we think differently, but also with our tendency to assume what others mean.

The politician says "the cat was not black" and the journalist or the 'opinion maker' says "he said the cat was white". No, he didn't say that, but you can see how people so easily make assumptions.

Always be aware that your words are not taken literally, people interpret your words but mostly, this is coloured by what coincides with their view. Any view they have on the subject will be used to temper and interpret your words.

We make assumptions about what we hear and then interpret it from there. Your friends are effectively interpreting their assumptions about your words, not your words directly.

How do we ever understand each other?

~~~

Love
28

"If love is the answer, could you please rephrase the question?" – *Lily Tomlin*

There can be little doubt that our friend, as I hope by now you have come to consider Albert to be your friend too, loves his Neerlee Faithful. Albert has been in love with his girl since he was a boy.

I thought perhaps at this point I could mention how he, in his unique way, showed his undying love by making this week's visit to Bunnings a special one for Neerlee. I do not recommend this as a future course of action, but this is what he told me.

"I do love my Sunday mornings at Bunnings, the smell of the exhausts, the glint of sun shining off the gas bottles, the wind blowing, the horn blowing and the gaggle of locals slipping in for a snag on the way to church. You just know, all is right with the world.

I promised Neerlee I'd buy her a new mower. The last one has been a bit hard for her to start for about a year now, petrol gushing out all over her thongs and the smoke was affecting her lungs, so I figured it was time to treat her.

This was going to be big so I had been researching the prices for about a month and, generous to a fault, I even said she could decide if this present was to be for her birthday or for Xmas. You should have seen the look of love in her eyes. I think it was anyway.

It's bloody terrible now, getting a park in the shade, the trade shed is getting harder every week and there's still no parking for Postie bikes. I'll have to speak to management about that one day.

Old Diamond was there as usual, lurking inside the trade doors, as he seems to do every Sunday, but I wasn't going to be caught out again. This time I remembered my discount shirt and I came prepared with my sunnies too. The reflection off his head is so famous I hear, people come all the way from Hervey Bay to Bunnings Bundaberg, just to ask old Diamond for directions to the toilets. A lot of them end up buying one too, I heard.

Well we found the cheapest mower all right, but in a fit of generosity, I decided to buy her the blue one. It's her favourite color, probably. Possibly.

She struggled a bit getting it into the back of the Leyland P76 with the cavernous boot, but when we finally got it home to our modest acreage in Titsupp Downs, I can't describe the excitement of opening the big box.

This was her first new mower so you can imagine I was pretty popular. And it was blue. She's pretty handy, my

Neerlee, only took her a couple of hours to put together and I even lent her a couple of my tools as she doesn't have much in the way of manly things.

I should mention Ralph. He lives next door and often comes over at night to do his business in our front yard, which I know is not very neighbourly, although we do get some green patches out of it.

They're pretty big ones too (not the patches) and if my Neerlee forgets to pick them up, well it goes hard and quite gritty. As it turns out, in her excitement on the first downhill run, the mower got away from her a bit and you guessed it, she hit a land mine at full rpm. The dust cloud was a sight to see and smell too I reckon. I'm not sure about that as I was having a bickie with my cuppa at the time but I reckon it was bad, judging by the way she ran around clutching her neck like she'd lost her pearls.

Quick as a flash I grabbed the hose and doused her down but I guess that just made it sticky because she became quite cross, probably with Ralph. She'll feel better tomorrow after she goes back and finishes the job and I'll be back in the good books. To be honest, I'm not game to ask and Ralph better stay home for while too I reckon. Time for my nap I think, after all that excitement."

~~~

Albert's ability to appreciate the complexities and connectiveness of the average woman's mind may be more stunted than those of his contemporaries but he gets points for trying, I think.

Let's put Albert to one side for a few moments and run our critical, practical eye over the subject and see if we can highlight it's most interesting components.

From poets to professors, philosophers to fishermen, singers to shoe salesmen, everyone has an opinion. Is there a subject more discussed and dissected, to which more attention has been devoted in prose, poem and song, yet in the end, what do we really know about love? How could I add anything to the discussion that has not already been covered?

Yet I hope my contribution to the word-avalanche improves rather than bloats the verbiage load, exceeds the poetic and gives a clearer insight and understanding of love. "Good luck with that" I hear you say.

Knowing where love comes from, knowing its history, knowing its uses, knowing what it is made of and how it evolved, will not change desire, however I for one, find understanding a subject, any subject, makes it easier to deal with, to reconcile and in some cases, to attain.

First thought though, is love not a noun at all, but an adjective, describing intensity? What evidence is there for love being a thing? I don't feel I'm writing about love, the thing, I want to understand how it works and how we deal with the intense pain it can cause us. Do we need love and while we're at it do we really know what IT is?

Before we can answer, we must establish which version of love we are discussing. What the poets and lyricists have failed to clarify is that love comes in two versions, familial and procreative, both with deep ancestral roots and which evolved for very different reasons.

Familial love.
Is a parent's willingness to sacrifice their life to save their child, love? If the answer is yes, then what do we call the act of a mother hyena fighting off a pride of lions that are intent on killing her babies? Is the act not the same and if so, is the name of the emotion driving this selfless act the same?

Even if we argue it is more about the animal protecting the passing-on of its genes, the same argument could be applied to the human animal so no traction there.

Essentially, the answer is 'yes,' what we can call familial love. As opposed to the fragile bonds of lusty love, familial love has incredibly strong bonds, almost unbreakable. We are tied to our close family by steel and to everyone else by string. Mothers to children, brothers and sisters, almost anything can be forgiven.

The evolutionary benefit of nurturing and protecting the young is so obvious it needs little more attention than to acknowledge it is so similar to human familial love, we can settle for the same descriptor. Given that we can do nothing about our relatives, let's look at the more capricious love of lust.

The Evolution of Lusty love
It costs us nothing to investigate in a few paragraphs evolution's claim on the origin of lusty love. There is clear evolutionary logic behind familial love, keeping the

family close for mutual protection and the preservation of one's genes, but romantic love? It evolved? Really?

It's pretty obvious that evolution, if it had emotions, cares nothing for the individual, only about the continuation of the species. Emotions generally, seem to have evolved as a means of furthering that goal. Nurturing and maintaining access to the future usefulness of other members of the group (friendship) needed a mechanism to ensure that individuals did all that was necessary to keep the conduit in a healthy state. Cue the entrance of 'love'.

The emotion we call 'friendship' that causes a sense of well-being or pleasure in the company of future useful individuals is one end of the string. What we call love, is the other end. Evolution's claim is that love is an emotion that exists purely as a motivator to maintain the species.

Being 'in love'
This occurs when two disparate (and yes, sometimes desperate) individuals are pushed together by primal urges or external arrangements, to produce more little humans. These bonds are moderately fragile but generally last long enough to satisfy evolution's demand to produce some little persons. While the passion can have a short life span, it's probably too cynical to accept the comedy version that says being in love is 'the best week in your life'.

The faint and faded pastels of acquaintanceship through to the vivid flush of love, it moves, it waxes and wanes, it disappears and reappears, all synchronously with time and proximity. An acquaintance is not someone for whom you feel a deep and binding love but they are on the same line, albeit a long way from central station. In time they may move up the line, probably first becoming a friend, then perhaps a close friend and confidant, possibly a personal relationship, it's a complex issue, but one constant is time.

We can lead a contented life without it, but having love in your life, makes happiness so much easier and better. So, is it just evolution at work?

The loss felt upon losing a loved one is a downside but of no interest to evolution as the pain suffered by an individual does not affect the survival of the species.

However, the slow dissolution of pain as time separates us from the departed loved one and the existence of the 'new-puppy-syndrome' makes sense if love is, at its core, an emotion conjured up by nature to keep us in touch with our future useful acquaintances, human or otherwise.

Whether love is an exclusive attribute of humans may always be in dispute but evolution does seem to have a good case at least. Of course, it does not matter in practical terms if romantic love is some magical gift only for humans or a natural product in the very real sense of the word, nothing changes our desire for receiving love in either form. The desire varies with individuals from the intense in some to a more lackadaisical attitude toward it in others.

This suggests, finally, an answer to our question, do we need love to lead a happy life? That answer is probably 'no' if we describe love as a thing but 'yes' by default if it's a measure of intensity of feeling towards others.

As you know, you can't make someone love you, but you can make it very difficult not to like you.

~~~

Trust
29

The way that trust is written about, usually gives the impression it's a 'yes' or 'no' issue and in a way, that could be correct.

I can trust a thief to steal at the first opportunity because trust is based on the evidence of past performance. The thief has stolen before so you can trust they will do it again. This is what makes it essentially different to faith where one has (or convinces themselves they have) faith in something or someone with no evidence or past performance whatsoever.

Just as a basic understanding of love, it's forms and life expectancy can be useful, so too an understanding of trust will help you in your quest for a sweet life.

It is important to realize that when we say we trust our partner, we know what we mean. Too often it means we hope and are confident they will be faithful, because as far as we know, they have been faithful so far.

The problem with trust is that it is very unlikely that a partner will always, in every instance, under all circumstances, even when influenced by recreational substances, act in a way that denies something to themselves and promotes your interests.

For the sake of our own sanity and protection, we should consider that our trust in our partner is realistic, that we humans come pre-programmed to consider our own needs first. It takes an effort of will, to deny ourselves for the benefit of another and it is to our credit, we succeed so often.

Trust is not a thing, it's a degree of certainty. Trust is the degree of confidence you have that someone will act a certain way. We hope they take or avoid actions that in certain circumstances, put our interests ahead of their own desires or needs.

When you think about it, is it reasonable to expect that someone will never, ever do anything to cause you pain? Having measured, reasonable trust, that people will act at some point, sooner or later, in their own interests, to satisfy their own desires or goals, is the acceptance of reality.

Betrayal and full control of your mind
If we can multitask, it is easy to believe we can think of more than one thing at a time too. It's one of many little tricks our minds play on us, leading us into thinking we can do things we can't.

If you are thinking about something pleasant, you cannot think of something unpleasant at the same time, but you can recall it a microsecond later. (That's literally one millionth of a second so we'd have to check that timing definition for accuracy.)

When you postpone the unpleasant for longer though, eventually your subconscious mind gives it a lower rating, much like the Google algorithm does when you search and suddenly advertising for that object pops up every time you log on.

Your mind does the same thing to you, so the smart option is to influence the outcome by putting the unpleasant out of mind, kicking it aside, replacing it with literally anything else. After a while, the unpleasantness gets a lower rating in your subconscious and it is put forward less often.

If you have been betrayed, tricked, conned, cheated, it is bad enough that you have been hurt. What is absolutely not OK, is being struck with the same stick over and over again. Every time you think of the injury, you are struck again, you are injured again.

When you are thinking of your shopping list or what you need to prepare for dinner, you are not being hit by the stick. Get into the habit of replacing the hurtful thought with anything you like, no matter how mundane. While you think of that, you are not being hurt again.

There is no suggestion that you can repress terrible events forever, never deal with them, but life is lived in the moment and if you are happy right now, does it serve some purpose to live long stretches in misery? If you have been betrayed, does that negative thought improve your happiness or detract from it?

Just like Google, you can keep getting reminders. You get to choose by replacing those thoughts that make you unhappy with almost anything else, and the negatives will lose their rating. This means they will get to reach your conscious mind fewer times. This really does put you in control.

The position of someone you love changes and if you are constantly reminded of some hurt that person has caused you, not only are you needlessly in constant pain, their place in your life is nudged further away from you and this is not in your interests. You need the ones you love close to you to help you keep your happiness.

You do not need to forever forget the hurt, the betrayal, the injury but neither do you need to be badgered with constant reminders of the hurt they caused. You don't even need to forgive them, although some say that is good for you too.
By understanding that we cannot think two things at the same time, we realise we have control. By simply

immediately changing your focus to absolutely any other thought, you devalue the importance of the injury and reduce the frequency it is regurgitated to hit you again.

Respect and Loyalty
Conclusions about the origin of romantic love does nothing to help us deal with the consequences of it. Assuming the union was not an orchestrated one, one thing for certain is that the first flush of romance will not last long. Nature has unfairly played with your emotions to get you into the sack but now nature cares nothing for your feelings once the defects in your new partner start to show.

Arranged marriages are still a thing, some even arranged with the consent of the parties to the marriage. Further, there are some marriages, more common than we think, where only one party to the marriage is 'in love' and the other accepting that it is a good plan they can work with.

It should come as no surprise that many of these marriages work so well, they last half a century or more. The reason this is possible is that the driving force of lusty love, only served to get the pair together and once that was complete, it was up to the couple to negotiate a lasting arrangement based on mutual respect. As a result, there are people who live long contented lives in a loving relationship who have never experienced being 'in love'.

Mutual respect is probably the single more important contributor to a long and successful partnership and this can survive many common failure points in a marriage. Respect for the other makes it possible to have loyalty to that person, however many mistake loyalty for fidelity.

It is common to read that a partner who has strayed, is disloyal, which is not necessarily true. Even if they have succumbed to temptation at some point, they can remain loyal supporters just the same. A loyal supporter is one who always has your back, supports you in the face of all others. Such a partner can be pure gold but if they have strayed, still deserve your anger.

The pain of discovering infidelity is a massive blow to trust and pride, aggravated by a feeling of foolishness for being naïve, but it does not mean that partner will now take the side of others against you.

Even a miscreant who has broken an agreement to be exclusive can still have future value to their wronged partner and certainly the prospect of forgiveness is a big future value for the offender.

If respect has diminished, however, that is a different matter. Partnerships, loving caring partnerships do not survive lack of respect and as there is no hope for the future, a dissolution is often the best solution for both parties.

Honesty
This is a very good thing in a relationship. Apparently. Complete honesty is a recommended path for couples to take. According to the American comedian Richard Jeni, "honesty is the key to a relationship. If you can fake that, you're in".

Jokes aside, complete honesty is not a recommendation

I endorse for two reasons, the first being that you risk causing pain to your potential life partner and second, no benefit is gained by making yourself so vulnerable. No one will love you more for having done it, so there is no net benefit.

Further, some people tend to relive painful memories, to their detriment. If your partner happened to be of that persuasion, the knowledge you provided could be a source of reoccurring angst, which in the long run works against you.

There is some wisdom in keeping some small part of you or your past, a secret. (A secret is a secret if you are the only one who knows. Beyond that, it's not a secret, it's just some bad news one hopes does not escape.)

Communication
Many people struggle with communication. I could take a risk and generalize at my peril, men for one reason and women for another. Don't pillory me too much for this but men know they are clumsy. They find communication annoying and dangerous too. If they must be embroiled in a discussion that explores deep-seated feelings, most know from experience it will probably end in tears and accusations of insensitivity.

Women on the other hand are not good at communication with men either, because men like things in easy-to-find boxes and just don't understand the complicated interconnectivity of everything.

TAKE AWAYS

Like friends, love comes in two versions, familial and romantic

Family bonds are extremely hardy.

Nothing good can come from a lack of respect for each other.

Trust is fine but it needs to be understood as a level of confidence.

Betrayal and disloyalty are two different things.

There is a good case for keeping some things to yourself.

A little honesty goes a long way.

~~~

Part four

Money

Making Easy Money
30

"I have enough money to last me the rest of my life, unless I buy something." – Jackie Mason

Anyone can make money. Making money is easy, so easy, even school-age kids at McDonalds can do it. Making a lot of money is a different task. The usual way we make money is selling some of our time, which is a good business model as we get the product for free. However, you can't make a lot of money this way because time is a limited resource. You only get so much and this limits the amount you can sell.

To arrive at financial security earning more is important but not the only lever. It is actually less important than spending less. To get best results, as you probably guessed, we need to do both. We'll get to that shortly.

To make more money you need to go further than merely selling your time to an employer. Think of other ways to provide a service either a highly valuable service to a rich few or a lower value service to many. When I say, 'service' that includes the service of producing a product and providing it.

If your ambition is to make a lot of money, you need to not only come up with a killer idea, but you also need money to fund the development and the delivery. In fact, you don't even need a killer idea, one of the old, tried and tested ideas will work fine, just so long as you have money to fund it.

Rarely, very exceptionally rarely (as totally redundant an expression as I can think of to make a point) an idea will pop up and if it pops up in your head and you happen to be lucky enough to be standing next to someone with large amounts of surplus cash and totally devoid of his own ideas, maybe, just maybe you will get your brilliant idea off the ground, after giving away a substantial slice. Better not to wait for that exceedingly rare event.

When I was young, trying to figure out what I was going to do with my life, the only thing we talked about was making money. We always needed more money to spend. If we could just make more money, we could spend it on all the things that would make us happy, plenty of good times with friends, cars, holidays, a big house, all the usual things.

I actually got pretty good at it in the end. This did not help me one bit. It wasn't until after I lost everything that I fully understood what I really wanted was to reach the **goal** of financial independence, not unceasingly chase the **method** of a huge income.

While I was concentrating on making more and more money, I should have been devoting a significant part of my effort on ruthlessly cutting costs until they came in under 80%. That would have provided me with surplus income, one of the primary ingredients of a sweet life.

At the time, I tended to agree with the sentiment that more income means you can spend more and spending more will make you happy right? Wrong. I spent plenty. In fact, I spent all of it and not because I wanted to either. I really was going about it from the wrong angle.

There are many ways of having a guaranteed, or semi-guaranteed income and they range from a casual job, a permanent job, to investment income, a pension, rental income to a full-on business-income.

To a large extent, the source of the income matters little. What matters is that it is semi-permanent. The only reason it is described as semi-permanent is that nothing in life is guaranteed and nothing stays the same forever. Everything changes to some extent, over time.

Full time work is where most people find themselves and it has the advantage of being able to provide enough to cover living costs, but it has one big disadvantage. Your employer is entitled to most of your normal work hours and this only leaves weekends and nights generally to make extra income.

The upside of selling your extra available hours is that usually, you get a much higher hourly rate than the discounted rate you have agreed to accept from a full-time employer.

There is something to be said for being self-employed of course, but it comes with drawbacks too. This was my choice, simply because of my attitude. When I was a young man, I was opinionated, confident (falsely so) healthy and rebellious. I found it difficult to accept a boss I considered unworthy, telling me what to do.

The drawback was that I had so little self-discipline, I was incapable of bringing myself into line. 'Self-employed' is also a separate trade and it has to be learned, just as any other trade. The drawback is learning on the job usually means the expected mistakes cost you dearly.

For example, a qualified plumber has a trade, but if he or she wants to go into self-employment, they have to learn the new trade and it is way more difficult to master than plumbing, engineering or maybe even being a doctor.

For what it's worth, I recommend a part-time approach to self-employment rather than immediately burning the bridge of employment. You can make a decision later about your future as a full-time or part-time employer of yourself and others.

Another reason for not opting for immediate full-time self-employment is the variation of weekly income increases the difficulty of maintaining and quantifying or checking on, a steady 80% level of expenditure. The accounting is quite difficult.

No matter how restricted, within reason, one can tick the box of semi-permanent income with as little as a government pension, as we were forced to do. Improving your position beyond that can be achieved by putting some effort into gaining a little extra income by selling one's spare time for an hourly rate. For those who believe they have nothing to offer, I can only say, "you are probably wrong".

If you are fortunate enough to live in one of the top 15 countries that provide good protection for their aged population, the Government will supply you with a modest pension. It may not be much, but if you have the other components outlined in this book, you can easily lead a contented life. I can attest to that.

I'm using the age pension here for demonstration purposes, but this applies to any sort of limited, but stable income. The total income is the important part, not the components.

If you happen to make a small profit on a second-hand mower you bought only to find you didn't need it and sold it again, well that's just a lucky windfall. It doesn't matter how you put together your total income and it is a fair argument that says a diverse income stream is safer than a single stream. After all, that has been the basic business strategy of investors and insurance companies for a very long time and look how that turned out.

There are many ways to make a little extra money and we will look at some practical ways and suggestions in the next chapter.

The lesson here is that the difference between rich and poor is essentially one of ***not spending*** and to get there, you need to sell as many hours as you can to ensure you have enough income to cover your **needs** and a little left over for your **wants** while developing the habit of feeling pain when spending and it works very well.

~~~

Bucket Filling
31

"There were times my pants were so thin, I could sit on a dime and tell if it was heads or tails." – Spencer Tracy

~

Not only does money flowing in help me have some left over, every time another packet hits my wallet, I get a buzz of pleasure as a bonus. This chapter is about how to find all that extra cash that is lying around, waiting for you. Money is all around you if you take the trouble to pick it up.

Everyone has a money bucket. You put money into it when you do something of value for a boss or someone else and money drains out the bottom whenever you buy something. Most of us start out finding a job and selling our time, which is a good plan to start with as we have little else to offer. As we mature, we develop experience to add to our knowledge base, which is acquired primarily on the job, with a contribution from our education which may also extend to a formal qualification.

So far so good but do we generally, steadily, acquire more wealth and financial security? Sadly, the answer is 'no' for most of us and there is no secret for this failure, we spend all we earn. The job becomes a price we pay so we can spend on our desires.

Each of us is responsible for ensuring we have sufficient income to meet our needs and the needs of those dependent upon us and we need to look at a job as just one source of income. There is little point in bemoaning the pay rate and railing against our boss and the system, no matter how justified we may feel when it has no practical effect on our lives. Better we adopt the concept of being responsible for our income and that selling our time to just one person or company is selling ourselves short.

You probably have some income already, most people do, even if that is a small amount from Government assistance. To increase the money-in, you need to sell some more of your time and when we start looking at our main job as just a part of our income, just one place where we sell time, it diminishes in importance as our confidence and independence grows.

When we make this effort and change our thinking this way, we begin to resent money flowing out the bottom of our bucket because one becomes acutely aware of the effort we are making, to put more money in.

This is where you can harness the power of habit. We develop and live with habits all day, every day, why not create some that could make you financially independent? The trick is to turn your powerful natural urges into powerful habits.

Two forces are at work in our brain that are so natural we underestimate their power and barely notice them — not wanting to spoil a record — and being bored with the status quo.

A powerful contributor to our mission success was something that happened a long time ago. Because it now comes naturally, I had not thought about it when first wondering why we were able to cruise to home ownership.

The Daily Net
Many years ago (about 1985 I think) I decided to keep a record of how much money I made for the week. In the beginning, I was working in one of my brief periods as an employee, filling in for a salaried manager of a window manufacturing company during his Long Service Leave. When he returned, I resumed full time self-employment.

I called this record-keeping effort the not-very-imaginative 'The Daily Net' and I used a day-to-a-page diary to record my net profit for the day. I calculated this by entering one fifth of the temporary salary I was being paid, plus whatever I earned doing other work after hours and on the weekend. The weekend work was mainly small handyman jobs and sometimes even regular office cleaning jobs. For jobs that took several days to complete, I'd allocate a percentage of the work done so far, the estimated profit I'd make, depending on how much of the job was completed at that point. As I finished, I'd put the balance of the profit to that day.

At the end of the week, I'd make three entries in the bottom right corner of the last day, the profit for the week, the total earned since I started and divided that by the number of weeks to get an average.

Two things happened that shocked me, literally astonished me. First, I found I was disappointed, very disappointed in fact, if the week's profit was less than the average and second, on the weeks that were above the average, I was not particularly impressed or satisfied. By the time mid-week came around, I became obsessed with the urgency to make enough profit to not spoil the record.

In the beginning I was making around $700 a week (this was 40 years ago and a fair bit of money then) but within a year, I was disappointed if I made less than $1425. I had become so used to seeing my results being a little more than the average to date, to have to enter anything less than the average, felt like an abysmal failure.

I had never had so much money in my pocket. I had to take money out of my wallet each week just so it would fit in my back pocket.

I could not always rely on profit from jobs to keep my average up, so for a long time I supplemented it with part-time jobs and selling anything valuable I could pick up second hand.

I would do whatever it took to avoid writing a lower figure in the diary, making me face my weakness or failure.

All this happened without any input from me except keeping the record, as if my life depended on it. In the background, my powerful urges were doing the heavy lifting, driving me forward to not spoil the record.

I never fully realized until much later why this worked so well. I was in the habit of entering every bit of profit within hours and sometimes within minutes of when it was earned. I never waited until the end of the week to enter my successes. It gave me instant gratification and because I was doing it many times a day, the habit took hold very quickly. Every time I found a way to enter a few dollars profit for the day, I received another hit. As a side benefit, looking at the page reminded me how well I was performing, motivating me to do even better, to break the record.
This was the powerful force of habit that drove me forward with no conscious effort from me.

Developing this attitude helps us both ways, increases our income, it has a dampening effect on our spending and encourages us to insist on good value for what we do have to spend. It's a win all round.

To get your bucket overflowing, there are three options, earn more, spend less or do both. We don't have to choose just one but all three together is pretty sure bet to work best. For the moment, let's talk about putting more money into the bucket.

Money is all around you, turn in any direction and you are looking at money. People have money to give you, all you need do is ask. These are not 'in-theory' ideas, they are not ideas that might work, they are ideas that I use every day, every week. They still work for me and they will work just as easily for you. There is nothing special about the way I make a few extra dollars.

~~~

Hiding Your Light
32

There is absolutely no point in being good at something if no one knows about it. Almost everyone has things they can't do or don't want to do but are willing to pay others to do for them.

There are many ways to advertise that cost nothing, including putting a sign out the front to advertise you are willing to hire out your trailer/van/ride-on mower/pressure washer or anything else you can think of. Even if this only earned you $100 in a year, that sign is helping you and it's so much better to have that $100 in your wallet than not, regardless of the boost it gives your feeling of happiness.

You can do some of your best advertising through social media, in local town, village or suburb groups where it costs nothing to let people know you have time on your hands and what you are capable of doing for them. Few of us have so little in life skills we have nothing to offer others. For example, even the least accomplished of us could probably deliver some leaflets for a local business.

You have capabilities whether you recognize them or not. The only thing you need do is tell others. One of the easiest ways to advertise is putting a post on your local community Facebook group or other local social media. This is no different to how people made money a hundred years ago, placing an advertisement in the local paper except that now, you can do it for free.

You don't need fancy graphics or an advertising guru, you just need to let people know you are available to do whatever it is that you can do. You have skills that you probably don't even think of as skills, but to someone, what you can do is useful and they will pay you, to do it for them.

Things you can advertise
If you hold the view that you are not good at anything, you are selling yourself short as there are definitely things you can do that some others can't, even if we are just talking about being able to drive someone to the shops, picking up an outdoor setting from Hardware, cutting the grass, cleaning a pool or walk around the yard and

pick up sticks. There is always something you can do that someone will pay you to do.
You can take up handyman/woman work and before you say I don't know how to do handywork, think about the things that you DO know how to do and it is not difficult to find a skill that someone, some time, will pay you for.

I suggest making a list of mundane things that you can do, that one day, someone may want you to do for them. You can start easily by simply writing down what you are doing as part of your routine, simple things. Not all of them are winners, but even the most basic actions are difficult or annoying for someone.
Other times you will see or read something that reminds you of a skill. Bear in mind that a large section of the population is over the age of 65 and many are keen to have someone handle irksome tasks for them.

Add it to the list and then advertise a couple of items from the list. It does not matter or mean anything if you get no immediate response but most times someone will react, often by asking if you happen to do something else that may or may not be on your list. If you think you can help them, add it to you list. If one person was looking for that, others may want it too.

New Skills
At no time in history has it been easier to acquire a skill that people will pay you for. You Tube is your friend and Mr. Tube knows all you need to know about almost every trick of every trade and is willing to share, if you are willing to learn.

You can learn how to do almost anything by watching a few videos and maybe a little practice. You do not have to be the best tradesman or woman in the world, just be able to solve someone's problem.

Just around the average house or unit, there are dozens of opportunities for fixing small problems, from resealing a leaking shower, replacing a broken tile, lubricating a sticky window, replacing the rollers under a door (you'll need some help and experience for that one) refitting a cupboard door or shelf, the list seems endless.

Once you have done one small job you have never done before, advertise it separately as you now know how to do it and eventually you become 'expert' in that one thing.

If you happen to be familiar with vehicles, there are dozens of opportunities to learn to do particular skills and the same goes for outdoor activities and gardens.

Opportunities also abound for those who can help people with basic computer problems like getting online, emails and websites.

If you own a light commercial vehicle or even a handy larger standard vehicle, people will pay you to pick up and deliver mulch or fertilizer or garden logs.

You may play guitar or some other instrument, people will pay you to come sit with them for an hour or two and show them a few tips and tricks at least. If you are really fortunate and have a second language, there are even more opportunities.

Advertise stuff you get for free
Other opportunities are also there if you are aware and thinking about earning a little extra. For example, many people give away some of their stuff when they are moving house. Others will accept much less than current value for stuff they just can't be bothered going through the sales process. Garage sales, Facebook Marketplace, Gum Tree are just some of the current sites that have free or nearly-free stuff you can sell.

Garage Sales and Boot Sales
Also known as 'yard' sale, 'tag' sale and 'moving' sale and by a few other names in the US and Australia, there are many motivations beyond 'moving'. In the UK and Australia 'car boot' sales are popular where people gather in open areas for the sale.

It pays to be attuned to the reasons behind the sale. For some, the least interesting to you, the seller just wants to make some extra cash and will be looking to get the best price. Other reasons are moving locally, moving interstate, divorce, partner death, retirement and downsizing.

Why is that important? There is a cost in getting to a garage sale and many are conducted on a Saturday morning, so for one thing, you don't want to waste fuel driving all over the area and secondly, you get the best results at certain sales.

When reading the advertisement or post (on Facebook Marketplace for example) one can tell something about the sale from both the type of goods and the wording of the ad and this tells us something about their motivation.

Sometimes the sale is not about making money, in fact often, it's more about getting rid of 'stuff' cluttering up their lives or not worth taking with them or they can't easily give it to charity. Basically, these sellers would just prefer their 'stuff' went to a good home and don't care about the money so much.

(I have even once been offered a treasured grand piano where the seller made it clear she didn't care about the money, just so it went to a good home. I could have had it almost free, but that would have been unconscionable as I did not have the right environment to keep it in good order and in any case, someone will have paid her at least part of its true value.)

If you come across as a professional, just looking to rip people off, picking the eyes out of the sale, you may be successful but it's a bit grubby.

Garage sales are a great source of cheap stuff and there are nearly always bargains to be had, but a bargain is only a bargain if someone else wants to buy it from you. You may already have some expert knowledge and many people who regularly make money for re-selling concentrate on their specialty.

I know a guy who paid for his nearly new 4WD doing that alone over a period of just two years selling much of it at 'car boot' sales and on Facebook Marketplace.

You just need to be the one who does not mind doing the leg work of selling. It can be tiresome but that's why you can get it cheap or for free. It can be fun too.

Part time work

You may already have a full or part-time job, but you have time available when you are not otherwise engaged. Part-time jobs appeal because you just have to turn up for work and you don't have to find someone else to pay you. Nor do you have to think about selling anything or finding customers or providing product. You just turn up, do your shift and go home, leaving all the hard bits to someone else.

The downside is you are at the mercy of someone else who has control of at least that part of your day, or night, and you may not like the work, work colleagues or the work environment so it becomes a real chore, an effort to go whether you feel like it or not.

The bottom line is the same as the introduction line, money is all around you if you take the trouble to pick it up.

~~~

Leaking Money
33

"The best way to double your money is to fold it in two and put it back in your wallet"

The takeaway from this chapter is that we need to find ways to reduce our expenditure to achieve an excess of income over outgoings. There are many ways to do this, however most of us are limited to a large extent by our income and cutting your expenditure in a high-cost area is often near impossible.

The answer seems ridiculously obvious as I write, to move to a less expensive area but this too can be very difficult. I know of no other way to get such effective results and seldom is a difficult goal achieved without some pain, so I am writing what I know. Your situation may make that exceedingly difficult right now, but planning costs little.

If understanding friendship is top of the list of skills that help create a sweet life, at number two must sit cost cutting.

Enjoying a sweet, relaxed, confident life depends so much on having surplus money, becoming an expert on this is a no-brainer. If you become an expert in controlling money leaking out, you can almost guarantee to have money you don't need and that my friend, is a fine thing indeed.

The best part is that money stopped from leaking is far **more valuable than money earned**. Yes, you read that correctly, **money not spent is worth more** and here's why.

Depending on the country, income tax mostly hovers around the 30-35% mark, so $100 not spent is equal to $130-$140 extra in your pay that week. Even if you are on significantly less than the average wage, you need to earn more than $125 gross (before tax) to have the $100 to spend.

It's like getting big pay rises for doing nothing but putting off spending something now, that you really don't absolutely need. People on higher incomes get an even better result, due to the higher tax bracket. **Not spending money is the single fastest way to get financial independence regardless of your income.**

You need to get good at cutting costs, so much more than making money. This is where making a lot of money is born. People who are good at cutting costs, have surplus money, no matter the level of income. They know that making a lot of money does not come from selling more hours, getting a higher pay rate, but from cutting costs.

If you have the fortitude to reduce overheads to suit the income, to spend less than 80%, you need only do that. If you have the skill or good fortune to increase your income, you only need do that, but this is never enough if uncontrolled overheads remain.

What happens to the working poor is that when income increases, the temptation to increase expenditure is too much and the much-desired positive balance, disappears once more.

The goal is 80/20, the minimum difference between income and expenditure. If you can get the best value for your time and you can cut harder, you accumulate faster, obviously. Consider these surplus funds as precious tools, tended and protected. They are the tools you need to make serious money. Without the tools to work with, no idea is good enough. A tradesman would never part with his tools and surplus funds are the tools with which you build a happy home, a happy life.

You may feel that you can't cut your costs any further and that may be true. If so, you just need to remember that when you increase your income, you must still keep this lever pulled all the way back. If you are making $1,000 a week and your costs are $800, you are doing well. If you increase your income by $200, the most you can increase your spending is $160 to maintain the 80/20 rule. (It's a math thing.)

If your prospects for increasing your income are limited and your spending is already cut to the bone, what can you do?

Move

The cost of living in most cities is substantially higher than in regional areas so it stands to reason that one of the ways to reduce your costs is to move. Aside from friends and family ties, there is one more reason to find this concept hard to handle, getting another job.

Given that your friends have no hesitation in leaving you behind when they get a better job-offer in another location, maybe you should consider this as an alternative for yourself.

We will address the ins and outs of moving to a cheaper area in another chapter but for now we just need to be aware that it is a course of action that has many benefits. Pour all your extra earnings into getting rid of debt. Do not be tempted to buy more stuff until the debts are cleared, starting with the super expensive credit cards.

When done, cut them up and get a debit card. Better still, get a debit card first then cut up the credit card. If vehicles have a large debt, sell them and buy a cheap replacement for cash only.

Sell anything you don't need to live. Keep the precious stuff certainly, but a lot of what we have is not required and you won't miss it.

Golden handcuffs

You've probably seen it before, the image of a monkey clutching a prize in a bottle, but the neck is too narrow to allow him to withdraw his hand. To remove his hand, he must let go the prize. Sometimes we have to let go so we live to fight another day.

The act of buying something you have always wanted generally gives one pleasure and most things of value come with an overhead, devaluation or responsibility.
For example, a nice vehicle or boat will not only have overheads in terms of maintenance, but you also have devaluation, which eventually will lead it to junk or at best, vintage status.

As objects and properties are accumulated, there is no diminution in total overhead, it remains the same at best or worse, expands to consume excess income but the enjoyment is a diminishing return.

No matter how rich one might be, the limiting factor is our brain, the problem being our capacity to pay attention. Humans can only do one thing at a time and only think one thought at a time.

While you can relish the thought that you are flying First Class and you can enjoy the champagne, you can't enjoy them simultaneously.

Despite what we may think, all human brain processing is done by rapidly switching between tasks. Just as it is impossible to think about two things at the same time, it is also impossible to enjoy two things at the same time. We might think we do, but we don't. We switch between them, concentrating on one, then the other and back again. We have to stop doing one, to do the other.

Here is the problem, the more toys, the more pleasure-givers you own, the less time you have to appreciate them individually. No matter how many toys we buy, we are limited by the time we have to savour them. To make matters worse, the overheads do not similarly take turns, they are cumulative.

Overheads are not limited, they continue to survive, prosper and grow in some cases, even when we've had little time to savour the pleasures. One can soon reach the point where the overheads, the things that need your attention, demand more time than you have available to enjoy your toys, which can only give you a short burst of pleasure anyway as you switch between them.

Even worse news, everything you own is handcuffed to you. They follow you on holidays even when you leave them at home. Whatever concerns, maintenance requirements, depreciation, payments and security needs, they are with you 24/7.

This is just another case where more is not better. To add to the diminishing return issue, familiarity diminishes pleasure. This is because to appreciate things we need to put them in contrast and the most striking contrast is not owning them.

It is counter-intuitive but limiting your toys in number, increases their pleasure potential and reduces your maintenance anxiety. Getting rid of toys, even giving them away, benefits most of us to a surprising degree.

The bottom line is that you must choose to master the 20% surplus and this is done by cutting costs first and last. It does not mean you are forever banned from having a pet, from owning a pool, living in a nice house or ever going out to dinner. It means you may have to put these on hold until you get into positive territory and the habit has become a way of life.

No matter where you live, the three biggest threats to your happiness are **pleasures, rent and credit cards.** We will talk about pleasure more a little later, so in conjunction with increasing your income somewhat, we can look specifically at what you can do about the other two.

~~~

Albert's Unfortunate Accident
34

My friend Albert is good at keeping costs down and he came up with a plan to buy some paint to upgrade the look of his toilet. Now this is not a course I would embark upon, maybe a new toilet is justified, but the thought is right.

Things didn't go to plan and he decided in the end to just go home without the paint, but I'll let him tell you the story.

"I was keen to get to Bunnings this Sunday. I needed some paint because our toilet bowl was looking a bit shabby and I reckon a coat of paint would be cheaper than buying a new bowl. We parked the '73 Leyland P76 with the cavernous boot in the shady 'Trade' section and after checking to make sure I had my sunnies, I led the way through the big trade doors.

Immediately I bailed up Old Diamond, the light from the overheads spotlighting his head like a heavenly shroud. Averting my gaze, I asked him for some tips about painting the porcelain.

As usual, he had some great advice, mainly that I should "go to aisle 21 and look for Mister Bit" who he assured me, would be able to answer any technical questions.

Well obviously Mr. Bit, the painting expert, was on a break and I decided to walk up and down the aisle for a while 'till he came back. After passing the lady behind the desk for the 9th time, I felt she looked a little queasy by the strange look on her face and I guess she was asking permission to go to the toilets because she was looking in my direction and whispering in the ear of her boss.

By this time I decided Mr. Bit was probably not working on Sundays and I went off to find my Neerlee and head to the café. There is a new staff roster there now, since I was banned, so I can probably sneak in undetected.

Until June 2020 I think it was, before I was banned, my Neerlee Faithful and I would go to the Bunnings café every Sunday morning so I could read Saturday's Newsmail and catchup on the obituaries. On this morning, just before she went to get my coffee and piklets, I mentioned that I would look in the paper to see if there were any ladies weight-loss classes advertised, you know, just to help her out.

Apparently she slipped on the way back and just as she got to the table, my steaming mug of long black slipped off the tray and ended up on the front of my stubbies. That's what started it.

I leapt to my feet, possibly loudly, and knocked over my chair and the one behind. Unfortunately the lady who was sitting on it ended up on the floor with her scones and jam plastered all over her and her friend, which she had carelessly pulled off her chair as she went down.

I was going to stop and help but by that time my Niagras had stretched to the size of overinflated footballs and I was in a rush to get to the toilets. People scattered as I ran towards the source of cooling water as I gently let them know there was some urgency in my need for clear passage.

Some guys. Honestly, as I was cooling myself in the basin, a couple of occupants looked at me like I was some sort of nutter but on the upside, my boys had reduced in size to look more like sunburnt avocados, which is what they usually do anyway, and my recent bout of Barcoo Rot was instantly cured too. At least everything looked the same colour although I don't think that colour has a name.

When I exited the toilets, Neerlee was waiting patiently, a quiet and gentle smile on her face, clearly she was relieved I was OK. We decided we could put off buying paint this week and headed straight for the trade doors, which as anyone who is familiar with Bunnings Bundaberg, is a long way to waddle.

While I tried to look normal and Neerlee pretended we were not together, it was clear from the kids hi-fiving me that they thought I was doing a Donald Duck impersonation as their frightened mothers tried to cover their eyes. If it wasn't for the water trail I left behind, you wouldn't have known I had just had a near-death experience.

Well, we didn't get any paint and you can't read the obituaries any longer, now that the Newsmail doesn't print any more, but at least they have forgotten about my ban and the coffee is still good.

As we left through the boom gate, I told Kenny Transplant, that's the nickname I gave him and I can tell by his expression he loves it, that he should let the management know that I wouldn't be in next week as I was going to visit the grandkids in Brisbane. To see the smile on his face, well, it just makes you feel good to do that to someone, put a smile on their face. I know he was happy for me.

I was going to tell the grandkids the good news I was coming down but I just had some really bad luck with that. Every time I've called, it turns out they were going away for the weekend too, so this time I won't tempt fate and just turn up. They'll be so excited, I can just see their little faces now."

~~~

Poison
35

"I was fine with selling my house cheap. The landlord, not so much."

As soon as one is old enough to 'leave the nest' you are expected to **pay rent to a landlord**. This is expected in society and I'm here to tell you, that is bad advice and to be resisted. If you are well past 'nest-leaving' and still paying rent, the time is now. You must stop as soon as possible.

This is not easy if you have children and are now caught in the rent trap where your income is not sufficient to save for your own home. There are things you can do to get out of the trap, including waiting until the kids leave home. I don't recommend that option.

Rent is without doubt, the most expensive and destructive expenditure you have. This is a tough nut to crack simply because we need somewhere to live, to sleep, somewhere to store our 'stuff'. It is unlikely you can eliminate rent overnight but you can work towards it, inch by inch, never letting the goal of 'NO RENT' out of your sight. To get out of the trap you need to do a couple of things which seem hard but are not as unpleasant as being old and poor.

Most of us will not be too pleased with the idea of renting the cheapest place in town and that's fair enough. A good reason then for moving to the regional cities and towns but maybe your pride has a hand in here somewhere.

Before we list the steps to take, we need to know the destination. What I will suggest is a 10-year plan to leave the city (if that's where you live now obviously) and return (if you care to) as a debt-free property owner. From that point, armed with the mental toughness picked up on this journey, you will be able to trade your way up to real financial independence.

If you are serious and interested, you could take advantage of the desperate need in country areas for willing workers, especially those with some basic skills and a desire for financial independence. This will mean uprooting your current life and that sounds scary I know, but better than waiting for the lottery to kick in.

If instead, it sounds exciting, you may be on the road to a much better, happier life. Even if the idea of moving to a low-cost environment is not for you, finding reduced rent will help and this may be achieved by moving to a lower standard, smaller premises or less attractive location, provided there is sufficient rental accommodation available to be choosy.

Although finding somewhere to sleep is the goal, a lot of

us go further than that, having a 'standard' that we demand which, if we are brutally honest, is really just the desire to have things we haven't earned yet.

If reduced rent in a city is unacceptable, that brings us back to moving to a cheaper part of the country where a higher quality of accommodation costs less and lower standards are cheaper still. This too is only temporary as less rent is not 'NO RENT'.

Another possibility is sharing the costs. This is a common way of addressing the problem, especially in the young just starting out on their own although, for most unfortunately, the benefit of reduced rent is more than made up for by spending the left-over money on 'party-time'.

The best we can say for these solutions is that they could be a temporary fix until a 'no rent' solution can be implemented.

For under 25 singles and couples, mobile accommodation is not out of the question. I've met one young guy who bought a bus and was travelling around the country with a mate, working in the building industry. Others have solved the issue by buying a caravan and sharing a power connection in a relative's back yard, sometimes paying 'rent' by mowing the grass or yard maintenance work in exchange.

We considered it too, when first looking at solving the problem after the company crash. As it turned out, the house sitting idea worked but that would not necessarily be easy or practical for a young working individual or couple.

There are variations on this theme, exchanging labour for rent and having accommodation that one owns is by far the best of these alternatives.

Young families may be able to use some combination of the mobile accommodation solution, but as the kids get older, a more permanent solution is required. If you have been sticking to the 80% rule, the solution could be to buy a block of land where the local council is more relaxed about temporary (mobile) accommodation. This rent-free period gives you more time to put up some form of permanent living arrangements. Owner Builder permits are easy to get.

Pre-teen and teenage kids, the job is so much harder because it is very difficult to keep expenses under the 80% mark and that means working longer hours to increase the income to keep the 80/20 ratio.

Not only do the longer hours limit time available for building your home, but mobile accommodation is not a good solution for teenagers for whom peer interactions and perceptions are all consuming. In this case, it is all the more important that the 80/20 rule apply so that a deposit can be put together for an existing house.

When looking at borrowing and buying, do not forget that while you are eliminating the rent problem you are taking on the insidious interest burden and the repayments must not interfere with the 80/20 rule.

Retirees

There are a few, like us, retired, but for various reasons find themselves sans home and renting as a consequence. As discussed at the beginning, we tackled the problem by moving around the country looking after the homes of people who had pets but wanted to take a holiday.

There were other options too that we considered and provided you are still physically able, you could consider the farm/light duties route or even just country towns that are crying out for population and workers, even part time workers supplementing their pensions.

You may be able to negotiate a number of cost reductions past just rent, electricity, gas, some food costs, garden vegs, eggs, Pay TV, even smaller items like cleaning products and some fuel expenses. There's probably more. For us, as I said, over three years, it was enough to build a small house.

If you are stuck with renting, at least avoid pools if you can. Renting a house that has a pool slows your progress even further. It's a double whammy, with rent being at least $100 a week more and running the pool adds another $15 to $20 a week, in just power costs alone.

~~~

Seduction 36

"Good to know, when the cashier says "strip down facing me" she means your credit card."

The thing about seduction is that, even if we like it, we know the seducer is primarily looking at their own needs or benefits. Maybe, if we're lucky, there is a benefit in it for us too.

The financial seduction of the young is set as soon as one is able to earn an income, sometimes before that and it's hard to avoid. The banks are keen to get the punters into debt with easy credit available for all the things you desire.

While credit cards and debit cards work equally well, it's the credit cards the banks want you to have. Maybe it is because they want you to have a wonderful life with all the trappings of wealth.

Maybe it's because they know that if they can get you to buy the things you desire without having the money to pay for them, they will make a handsome profit. My money's on the latter.

For most of us that have fallen into this trap, getting out is extremely difficult. How often have we heard the plaintive cry "as soon as I pay off my credit card, I'm going to take the scissors to it and cut it up". This rarely happens. I've got a better idea. Why not cut it up today? By the time your debit card arrives, you may have some money in the account of your own to spend.

If you can handle the three big happiness killers, rent, gratification and credit, you can just about guarantee a financially secure life.

One of the great seduction lines goes "live for today, you may not be here tomorrow." I'm going out on a limb here, but I promise you that you will be here tomorrow and it will be better without the debt.. (If I'm wrong, I'll apologize.) Some other popular lines are "you only live once" (that's true) "a little of like is good for you" (maybe but not relevant) "life is meant for living" and so on. The point of these lines is for someone to get their grubby hands on your money, not for your benefit.

Your pet project
What could be more seductive than those puppy dog eyes? Combined with a credit card that has not yet reached its max, the combination is almost irresistible.

Buying or adopting a pet seems like a good idea, providing companionship, improved mental health and sometimes, exercise. How many young people just starting out, sign up for all three, rent, credit card and pet?

They're not cheap and many of us tend to overdo the expenditure just a little. For example, more than one third of US dog owners give their pet birthday presents and almost as many admit to having employed professional photographers.

Sixty percent of Australia's eight million households have a pet. In the first year, costs are especially high with initial expenditure up to $3,000 for registration, microchipping, health checks, accessories, veterinarian, pet insurance and medication. If the animal is adopted, subtract the purchase cost.

After the impact of the first year, according to the RSPCA the average annual cost is $1627 for a dog and $962 for a cat. Given that there are 29 million pets and only 8 million households, that means a lot of people are paying out a lot of money for companionship. Admittedly this number includes all types of pets, not just companionship pets. The Australian average household has a gross income in excess of $100,000 in 2022.

It should come as no surprise that 35% of pet owners live on an annual income of less than $50,000.

High costs and a low income do not sound like a good starting point for winning a sweet life lived in one's own home, even if you already own the home.

Two or three-pet households are common and in view of the expenditure, delaying pet ownership until after one is financially independent seems like a good strategy, especially considering the delaying effects of losing $3-

5,000 a year. A two-year delay could cover the deposit on a block of land in its own right with no other cost cutting involved.

While we are on the subject of cost, it's worthwhile just reminding ourselves about the meaning of these common words we know so well.

Cost, loss, expense, expenditure, outlay, we use these words as though they mean the same thing although that is far from the truth.

Cost is loss, pure and simple, not investment. For example, I can tell you how much my old car cost because I can see the difference between what I paid for it and what I received when I sold it. THAT was its cost.

When someone says, "nice 'whatever' how much did it cost?" you know what they are really asking about is how much cash you exchanged for it. You can't answer the question literally because you still have it. Only when the asset is turned back into cash can you answer the question.

Obviously, we are simplifying here as there are other matters to consider, with vehicles for example, not the least of which are deprecation and running costs. The point I'm making is that it's good policy to keep in your mind the difference between cost and investment. Cost is loss.

When we're talking about a service, like hiring someone to clean the pool or clean your house, we are indeed justified in using the word 'cost' because we exchanged our money for no tangible asset.

If we spent a thousand times more buying a house, it cost nothing, because we still have the money, just in a different, albeit less convenient form.

Expenditure, expense, is slightly different in that while it is also a cost, it can better be understood as a necessary loss of cash to achieve a goal that overall, increases the amount of cash you had before you incurred the expense. For example, a factory's power bill is a necessary expense to make a profit doing other things.

There is no problem with going along with the crowd using the word 'cost' when people mean 'outlay' but the point is, we need to be in the habit of viewing 'cost' as 'nothing tangible in return'.

We are seduced into thinking that credit is a safety net and for that reason better than a debit card, so they will always be with us, but for what it's worth, I'd recommend giving a thought to determining if normal use of the card is for a cost that will deplete you or for an exchange, something you can turn back into cash.

~~~

Temptation
37

There are so many areas of our lives that require managing temptation, it's hard to know where to put the methods of dealing with it. It affects our money, our relationships, our control of our attitude, just about every aspect of our lives is subject to the subtle seduction of temptation.

As credit cards so often make it hard to resist temptation, this seems as good a place as any to address it. If you are in pursuit of a sweet life, this is another skill you must at least become reasonably good at.

One of the better ways to deal with the torture of temptation is to physically change the proximity of the temptation, either by moving it or moving ourselves. For some things, it's easy. If you are prone to snacking on chocolates or scotch or whatever you know you need to change, don't buy them, don't look at them, don't have them in the house. Whatever it is that is holding you down, start by getting it as far away from you as possible. You may have heard 'they are all around you so you have to learn to deal with it, so it's ok to have it in the house where you can exercise your self-control'. Bad advice when you fail and feel the psychological effects of failing once again.

I don't make comment on recreational drugs beyond the obvious, there is an increased personal risk if for no other reason than in many jurisdictions, they are illegal. That aside, the cost is horrendous and that alone is reason enough for me to pass.

Temptation is so often appealing to our desire to self-gratify. To take pleasure. We will deal with that and happiness shortly but for now, we just need to know, temptation is just our desire.

Sometimes contact with temptation cannot be avoided. Probably the best way to deal with that, until you can put a lot of distance between you and the temptation, is postponement.

One of the useful strategies used for dealing with addiction is postponement. Addiction and self-gratification have more than a little in common so it is not surprising that methods for dealing with cravings work equally well on strong self-gratification desires.

Children have come up with some wonderful ways to deal with strong desires. You may have seen experiments with kids where they are left in a room for a short while, sitting at a table, upon which an enticing sweet/cookie is sitting on a plate. They are promised TWO if they wait 10 minutes.
It is fascinating to watch as some succumb to temptation and eat the offering the moment the adult leaves the

room, while others endure the minutes ticking by, torturing themselves, gazing at their desire. The ones that handle the situation best are those the distract themselves, counting the legs on the chair, gazing under the table, looking at the walls and avoiding looking at the clock or the plate and its temptation. There is a lesson here for us.

If you really want to buy something you don't need but would be a pleasure, be it a new car, a chocolate bar, motorbike or a bottle of booze, postpone, postpone, postpone.

Put off the decision. Tell yourself you will make a final decision later, in 10 minutes or this afternoon or tomorrow or even next month, depending on the situation. It will surprise you how often a postponed decision softens your desire and fades somewhat after just a day or so. After a few weeks, even the most intensely desired object can fade dramatically.

What you should **not** do is torment and torture yourself as this nearly always leads to surrender followed by the damming feeling of failure that goes with it. Until you have surplus money that is not required for you or your family, don't look at brochures, don't join that Facebook Group, put it in the background until tomorrow. Be like the smart kid, use distraction to your advantage.

Giving in to temptations had some evolutionary advantages, the highly motivated risk takers producing more little persons like themselves, despite potential 'death-by-annoyed-father' but evolution won, albeit at the expense of many individuals. Not much has changed and in the modern sense, failing to postpone gratification still creates some terrible outcomes for the individual.

Most temptations don't result in death or disaster, well not in the immediate time range, but repeating the urge to buy, to self-medicate with pleasurable goods and services, eats away at our reserves or worse, stops us from creating reserves in the first place.

Clearly, most of us don't want to live like a monk and have no pleasures. Fair enough and there are ways you can get at least a little of what you like and still control your financial goals. Booze for example offers a few possibilities, provided of course, it is not the primary cause of your unhappiness. If you are a modest consumer and don't go on benders, binges and have blackouts, far be it for me to suggest anything that might deprive the Government of tax revenue. However I have noticed there are Facebook Groups and forums with thousands of members who will happily relate their path to enjoying $5 bottles of Bourbon and other interesting drinks.

For those who enjoy a beer of two, there are no end of home brew forums. I'm not making recommendations here, just making a note of public knowledge that might interest you on the way to cutting your expenditure.

The most common financial destroyers are
- retail alcohol, tobacco, pot and other drugs
- credit cards, clothes, shoes, handbags
- tattoos, eating out / take-aways
- pets, new vehicles, pay TV
- beauty and fashion, shopping expeditions concert tickets and subscriptions

~~~

The Gambler
38

"My gambling is only a problem when I'm losing."

There's a friendly use of the letters in the word 'gamble' which is claimed to stand for Give Away Money Because Losers Expect (to win) but maybe I made that up. I'm absolutely sure though, there are few more certain ways to sabotage a financial plan, than to gamble.

I don't mean the occasional lottery ticket, I'm talking about playing with the pernicious predators on your future, the companies that run the gambling 'industry'. At the risk of offending, there is nothing dumber than giving your money to a company that is specifically set up to return a maximum of 80% of what you give them.

The owners and operators of gambling assets are not gambling, they know the outcome. Only the punters are gambling and mistakenly believe, they can win. All the systems are tweaked to give the gambler no chance of making a profit and many enhancements created to entice you to stay longer, bet more, in the full knowledge that you will lose it all if you stay long enough.

When it comes to sports betting, men, especially those under 45 years, are at least twice as likely, to give their money to the bookies, but gaming machines seem to appeal to men and women equally.

Some become addicted to the dopamine hits. Just under 3% of Americans are addicts and suffer the side effects, not just financial stress on them and their families, but mental health problems (like depression, anxiety, and substance abuse disorders) all the way up to suicide.

Australians are some of the world's worst gamblers, losing an estimated $1,500 for every man, woman and child in the country, more than half of which goes down the throat of electronic gaming ('slot') machines. New Zealand, Canada and the US lose $495, $393 and $325 per head respectively. (That's in Australian dollars but you get the idea.)

When you consider that only 15% of Australians gamble regularly, it makes the extent of the losses rather impressive I think. Government statistics claiming that a quarter of them 'have a problem with gambling' is like saying Pavarotti could sing.

While everyone 'knows' you can't win on the pokies that does not seem to hinder the Australian enthusiasm for cuddling up to near quarter of a million machines, which happen to be located 94% of the time, in 6,000 clubs and pubs in low-income areas. Coincidence or what?

Here's two more interesting facts for you, more than half of regular gamblers smoke, a rate 3 times higher than the general population and 40% also have at least one other substance dependence.

Tax on smoking in Australia is so high, as of 2022, many smokers were paying $1,000 a month and suffering social isolation to feed their habit. A month.

Are you starting to get the idea that I have a less than favourable view of the 'industry' as it is so absurdly named?

Fortunately, gambling does become less prevalent as people age and that might have something to do with people becoming a tad tired of giving their hard-earned cash to a machine that only plays loud noises by way of a 'thanks for your donation'.

So why do people gamble, knowing full well they are going to lose? According to the boffins, there are two reasons, fun and misery. The fun bit is "stimulation resulting in increased dopamine levels". The misery is "dulling the pain of loneliness and/or negatively reinforcing relief or escape from stress or negative emotional states". Well, there you have it, explained. Not.

Let's face it, we gamble to make money. Actually it allows us to fantasise in public without getting arrested. The prospect of winning large, gives us the chance to dream about a windfall and its effect on the 'pleasure' aspects of our lives. Even the small wins are exciting, making the prospect of playing longer getting us closer to the big payday. That and it distracts us from reality;

little things like responsibilities, demands, work, confronting problems and other annoyances.

Hotels, clubs, casinos, they know what turns you on, makes you comfortable, allows you to suspend reality for a time, long enough to get your money, which is obviously the point of it all. They offer a range of entertainment options, food, alcohol, live music and shows, all the while simulating genuine social intercourse.

We help them, with our own cognitive limitations. Who doesn't think that a win is due following a series of losses? Or what about cognitive regret "if I quit now I'll miss out on the big win that is soon to arrive"? Worst of all, cognitive entrapment also known as chasing losses. "I can't quit now, I've lost too much."

At the very beginning of this book, I described my worst encounter with the Sunk Cost Fallacy, the "I can't quit now, I've put so much into this" thought process. Not only was it futile, pursuing something that was not headed in the right direction, I lost six precious years of the Sweet Life and I'm not even a gambler. Gamblers lose, it never heads in the right direction so for people who like to gamble, just be aware of the insidious trap of chasing your losses, aka the Sunk Cost Fallacy. You don't have to chase your losses, you can just quit and that part **does** lead in the right direction.

Calling gambling a 'game of chance' is a cruel joke, played upon the gullible. There is nothing left to chance in gambling but the words evoke a sense of fun, random luck smiling upon us and often, a sense of inclusion.

Money, the thrill of the chase, increased dopamine, all good reasons for starting to gamble, but why do some not be able to quit while they are behind? Why keep doing something that is no longer a pleasure in a system designed for them to lose even more?

Dopamine is released in the brain during pleasurable events, like eating, sex, drugs, all the fun bits, but a bit weirdly, it is also released by uncertainty. In gambling, uncertainty is the main game, one never knows for sure how the cards will fall and we can overdo the dopamine just a smidgin especially as it hits its peak in the moments leading up to a potential reward.

Aside from losing all your hard-earned, the other big disappointment of gambling dopamine is that like repeated exposure to drugs, repeated uncertainty produces lasting changes in the human brain and I have it on good authority, that is not a good thing.

When uncertainty is paired with lights and sounds, the urge to play is stimulated. By changing the frequency, length and tone of the sounds of jackpots, you can easily be misled into thinking there is more winning, than losing going on.

This is especially true in the modern electronic machines that offer several lines of bets that encourage you to play many games at once. The way it works is that some of the bets will be winners and they get the full treatment, misleading the player to feel they are winning and ignoring the losses. You win on some lines, lose on the others. Even when you win, you lose but the lights and sounds of victory convince you, you're a winner. Yay.

Their next trick is even more insidious, exploiting the 'near-miss' fallacy. Most machines now have a higher than chance result of 'nearly all' the reels lining up and tricking the player into thinking that in a few more plays, the winning combination will come up. Perversely, almost winning triggers a more intense urge to continue playing than actually having wins. Instead of losing, you're 'nearly winning'. Doesn't that feel better now?

If we pass on the machines for a moment, we should mention a trick used by the sports and casino hustlers, creating the illusion that although you lost this time, your performance was better than the average Joe. It's a form of flattery designed to get you back when you've got more money to give them. One thing common to all gamblers is the convenient memory. Technically it's called ***recall bias*** and it allows one to remember the wins and cheerily erases those inconvenient losses.

Those of us who find the prospect of losing $10 far too painful to even consider the benefit of winning $100, are fortunate indeed.

~~~

Methods vs Results
39

I read once (in 1972 I think) that successful people are driven by results. It is their primary interest, they completely, utterly focus on results. They don't care if they must sacrifice, they don't care if pleasure is postponed, they don't care how much effort they are required to make. What they care about is the result. These people are mentally tough, mentally muscular and ripped. If you could see their mental muscles, you'd not be surprised to see rust, they are so tough.

Contrarily, the average person, if indeed such an animal exists, is driven by methods, pleasant methods, easy methods, intuitive methods, even methods that don't work but require little effort. The real 'tough guys and girls' don't really care if the method required is hard, just whether or not it will produce results.

Some are only prepared to do what they enjoy, others will only do work that matches their qualification and others refuse to consider even postponing favourite pleasures and that is fine, albeit a grim outlook for future success. This book may not be of much help as it is about 'results and how-to-get-them' not 'results and how-to-get-them-by-pleasant-and-easy-methods'.

So many of us look at the method and if it's hard, look for an easier method and if that fails, give up on the result. Our first decision must be to choose whether from this point forward, will we be driven by pleasant methods or pleasant results. Pick one, they seldom if ever arrive in the same opportunity pack.

Procrastination
It is difficult to avoid postponing jobs we would rather not do. It seems the most successful way to get past it, is to choose the smallest possible part of the dreaded job and just do that bit. While you are on a roll, take a second tiny step and if you can gather the strength of will, a few more.

Then write down what parts you've done and identify the next step. When you do finally get to confront it, you'll have some track record of achievement and the psychological boost that part of the job has been done already. It's playing a trick on your own mind, but it works. At least if we know that it's just a by-product of something we can fix, the exercise of our self-discipline, then at least we make a start.

The idea of asking ourselves if we want good methods or good results nearly always prompts the question "where can I find a shortcut for this self-discipline gig? There's got to be a way to get the results an easier way."

You may have seen the joke sign in the bakery "I want buns of steel, but I also want buns of cinnamon".

As we read about financial seduction, shortcuts are traps, just as surely for doing hard tasks as they are for buying on credit. Taking shortcuts, trying to get what you have not earned, trying to find the easy, effortless way, wastes your time.

Retailers offer a shortcut to things you think you want now, so you end up with a lot of stuff you really didn't need. Paying for that makes an enormous difference to the time it takes to rightfully possess what you have earned.

Everyone in the finance business knows that people are easy to make money off by offering them a shortcut, albeit an expensive one. It's an old, tried and true way to make money, dating back thousands of years and to this day, the motivation, insisting on possessing what you haven't earned is still as strong as ever.

There are few shortcuts in this world and even if you find one that works, often the satisfaction of possessing the desired object is diminished and devalued by the ease with which it was acquired. Inheriting for example, is fine but in no way gives the same happiness, the same confidence, the same overall satisfaction as exercising your will and your power to earn it for yourself.

The desire to find an easy way often comes up when you are undertaking a task and an observer comes up with the question **"Wouldn't it be easier to….?"**

If you get asked this question a lot, either you are a total incompetent or you are one of those who prefer to do quality work. It is actually a form of that most annoying event, receiving unsolicited advice. As though you needed more useless crap in your life.

There is nearly always an easier way to do almost everything and sometimes an easier way is just what you need. However, the question often means that the person asking, just likes to do the absolute least work possible. Doing the job well is not high on their agenda.

What they are doing habitually is looking for shortcuts, finding an easier way, not with the goal of being more efficient, but with the goal of doing less work, even if the quality or the outcome suffers. It can be annoying too as it infers you have not thought of it, despite the fact it may be blindingly obvious and you have chosen to do it this way for good reason. Try to have patience with the person who's always asking, "wouldn't it be easier to....?"

This lesson, learned so many years ago, has been part of my DNA now for so long, I had simply forgotten the desire for good results was what gave me the power to achieve the outcome I wanted. A home and a sweet life..
Pleasing methods just never got a look in.
Having this tool in your kit will bring you more benefits than just about any other.

~~~

Part Five

Own Your Home

If we are right about our rating of friendship, cost cutting, results over methods, as the most critical <u>skills</u>, the tools needed to achieve the sweet life, there is little doubt in my mind that this <u>goal</u>, owning your home outright, is by far, the most important.

Moving
40

"Your time is limited, so don't waste it living someone else's life. Don't be trapped by dogma – which is living with the results of other people's thinking." – Steve Jobs

In this chapter I use some Australian examples which are convenient for our purposes because of Australia's unique situation. The country is like the US and Europe yet simplified by virtue of having a clear distinction between densely packed capital cities and sparsely populated country areas.

It is not practical to give examples from every country in every currency. The principals are the same. A US dollar in the US, buys about the same as an Australian dollar buys in Australia although it's not that close for the UK pound or Euro.

The same applies to land and house values, there are differences between countries, but the principals are the same. There's no need to consult currency fluctuations or foreign exchange rates to work out differences.

'Regrets, I've had a few, but too few to mention.'
These words are from that famous Frank Sinatra song, 'I Did It My Way' and although the words have great appeal, most of us indeed, have more than a few and some of them get a lot of mention.

All the matters we talk about will essentially come down to being independent and that can most easily be achieved by owning property, so of course we will be talking about owning your home. However, that's just the beginning, we really should be aiming for more than that, to give us true independence.

Pick any older person and ask about the property they could have bought, years ago for a great price, but didn't because, well, they didn't. They will almost always have a story of what they could have done, but didn't. If almost ALL older people regret not buying property they instinctively knew was a good thing, why would you repeat their mistake?

No matter how you are situated at this very moment, we need to remind ourselves that everything changes, every day, just a little.

The excuses we oldies give may vary a little, but mostly we acknowledge we could have managed the purchase but didn't for spurious reasons. If you dig a little deeper, the reason was mainly because it would have needed our taking some risk and we lacked the confidence or insight. Most of us were also cash-strapped due to the regular purchase of life's seductive luxuries, booze, tobacco, pot, whatever.

What massive value would those properties have for us now? Those luxuries seem so trivial looking back, self-gratification that only lasted a few moments, exchanged for property and prosperity that lasts a lifetime. Every time they will tell you that they could have done it, but.... they didn't.

Inaction regrets are the hardest to bear and they come up so often in conversations over a couple of drinks.
If you DO buy, try to avoid selling or you may join us in our 'regrets, I've had a few'. The best advice you will ever receive from someone whose future is behind them is, buy, hold, move along.

Why are you here?
That is not a philosophical question, rather an opportunity to think about what caused you to live exactly where you do.
The question might more properly be "Why do you continue to live here?" Have you chosen this place or have you just washed up here like driftwood or deposited here by parents who did not seek it out either?

You really don't have to live in an environment where you handicap your chances of being happy. There are countless places in most countries where conditions are good and have opportunity. Postponing in the hope that matters will improve, seldom results in a positive outcome and all too often in disaster. I understand that it is difficult, particularly where children are involved, but it must be done and now, not later.

There are many suburbs or areas that most of us will never be able to afford. Just because you grew up in a neighbourhood, does not mean you either must live there, that you are automatically entitled to live there or that life is unfair because you can't afford to buy a house there. In many cases they were not expensive areas even one generation ago.

But I LIKE living here
Fair enough but we generally need to earn the things we like, and in any case, it is a lot easier, necessary even, to appreciate something when you have contrast. No matter how wonderful a place can be, it does not take long for the wonderful to become the mundane. You'll appreciate it a whole lot more when you have lived elsewhere for an extended period.

For many people living in an expensive environment, they can develop an overwhelming sense of frustration and hopelessness. How can someone on modest wages, with or even without dependents, ever hope to save enough to put a deposit on a house?

I suggest that saving up a huge deposit on an expensive house in an expensive environment is not the most efficient way to move forward. The dream of getting one's name on the deed, 'owning' a house, completely overlooks, perhaps ignores, the fact that merely signing up to a lifetime of interest and principal repayments, is a long way from a financially-secure, contented life with money in the bank to spend as you please.

Obviously, it can be done that way, especially for those on high incomes, no children and a lot of discipline. If you don't qualify for all the foregoing, then why not consider a better, in my opinion, alternative?

Many people believe that it is difficult to leave friends and family and the movies reek with hackneyed phrases. Even 'The Piano Man' sings "if I could just get out of this place". With the rapid advancement of communications, leaving one's friends and family is hardly even possible anymore or at least it seems so, as you can be in constant contact, sometimes more so than when living in the same city.

Leaving used to infer there was a strong likelihood of never seeing someone again. In this century, that is a highly unlikely outcome. We can therefore, rethink the idea of 'leaving', putting it more on a par with 'long vacation' than 'never-see-you-again' and there are huge benefits in doing so.

As we discussed earlier, cutting your expenditure in a high-cost area can be exceedingly difficult if not impossible, so indeed the answer seems ridiculously obvious.

Most changes are forced upon us, so we react and adapt. Pick the path of moving as though it were forced upon you. It's never the right time. Don't wait for everyone to agree with you because that will never happen. Nearly everyone you know will pick sticking to the usual routine, even a boring or unhappy existence over uncertainty. Moving anywhere is the poster boy of uncertainty. You'll have little competition.

Don't just think it, write down the worst possible scenario if you lost your job tomorrow. Underneath write how you would change your finances and expenditure to cope and how you would repair the damage to your current lifestyle.

Write down these questions "what's the worst that could happen if I move?" and "what are the possible benefits if the move is successful"?

After you have written an answer to both, make a list of things you are good at, your strengths. Don't bother about fixing your weak spots. You only need to be good at a few things to be very successful in life.

Question. What is the most likely thing that will stop you? Hint: it's the most expensive product on earth

~~~

Pride
41

"It's not death a man should fear, but he should fear never beginning to live." – Marcus Aurelius

One of the two things that stops more people from being contented is the inability to control their pride. People lose fortunes for pride, lose family, even forfeit their lives for pride. To what end, what benefit you may ask. This devil is inside you too.

As mentioned in the chapter 'Self-Confidence', Bruce Lee the legendary martial artist, philosopher and filmmaker (1940–1973) said "***Pride is a sense of worth derived from something that is not part of us***".

That so often means our vanity, our perception of our status, in the workplace and or the general community. Our vision of our importance and standing is rarely in tune with the vision of those around us. We see ourselves as an important component, they see us as someone temporarily occupying a space.

This misreading of our significance so often leads to angst about the opinion of others to the extent we stop ourselves from acting in our own interests and in some cases, to even fatal consequences.

Resistance comes too from the family, including children who would just 'die' of shame if their parents can't provide them with (*here insert whatever trinket is in vogue*).

Even if you build up your strength and dominate self-gratifying expenditure, pride may be an even tougher opponent. Pride is a hungry beast and its favourite food is a plate of self-doubt and garnished with a splash of thin self-esteem. The power of your self-esteem comes from your merciless exercise of power over yourself.

What will neighbours, friends, enemies, business competitors, work colleagues, employers or family members think if you downsize, get rid of the expensive car and stop socializing every weekend?

They will not think, at all (about you anyway). They will consider it momentarily and then go back to thinking about themselves and worrying about what you think of them. You can sacrifice your future for nothing more than worrying about what others think, when they are only concerned with themselves and don't really care one way or the other, where or how you live. And for that, you could blow your chance to be happy. That is not a good deal.

You may be thinking now, 'I don't care what others think'. It's one of the little lies we tell ourselves, that we don't care. We most certainly DO care and that emotion is so powerful it can be fatal. It most certainly has the ability to make and keep us poor.

If others have an expensive house, cars and toys, we tend to automatically compare ourselves, making it about us as people, rather than on our performance and worse, we rarely even look for the facts, about how they came by the expensive house or what debt they have sunk into.

We look to ourselves and feel embarrassed. This can drive us to achieve but it most likely will drive us into debt to avoid a fear of 'what people will think'. You will never be free until you let go of your precious pride, your weak spot, that easily attacked and manipulated, self-manufactured substitute for self-confidence.

You must have as the first goal, a property that you own. When you are asleep, it does not matter if the property is a one-bedroom shack or a 15-room mansion. What matters is that you are not supporting a landlord.

You know what you must do, cut your overheads to the bone and make no secret of it. Boast of your control, your power, your self-confidence and your self-discipline. None, absolutely none of your family or friends, will have your strength of will and in very short order, you will have money in your pocket and most disinclined to let it go.

Buying affordability
There is quite a bit of difference across countries in the affordability of homes and is most easily expressed by matching income to housing prices. It can also be achieved a little more obliquely by comparing mortgage to income as a low mortgage average indicates the

original cost of the home is low.

In 2021, one of the easier places in the world to own your home is the US with an affordability rating of 3.4 (easier only for citizens in Saudi Arabia at a massive 5.1) yet only 25% of Americans own their home outright.

Outliers in the statistics can occur when there are wide differences in income levels. The USA is one such situation where there are many high-income and many low-income families. The low cost of homes does not help. We have the strange situation of having a country with low house prices and low ownership rates simultaneously.

At the other end, we have countries with exceptionally high ownership rates, Lithuania, Bulgaria, Croatia for example all above 80% and Romania on an eye-watering 95% ownership (despite an affordability worse than the UK). These anomality's have various causes and due in part to population mobility, emigration and other regional factors.

More to the centre we have countries like the UK where homes are expensive, so the affordability is a low index number, but the ownership rates are substantially higher than say, the US.
Canadians do better than the US in outright ownership at 30% despite an affordability index of only 2.02.

Australia has about a 30% ownership rate, similar to Canada, but at a disheartening (for first-time owners) 1.94 affordability which is a little easier than the UK but tougher than Canada and very much harder than in the US.

If you are already or about to be a highly paid professional with a salary several times the average wage, it should not be too difficult for you to save money for a deposit at a rate faster than prices are rising, assuming they still are (rising) as you read this.

Should you be half of a highly paid couple, the future house prospects for you are bright indeed. The same thing applies if you have hit upon a brilliant business idea in an area of high demand with existing and or future profits far above the average wage. You too can skip this chapter.

In either case, even if you live in an expensive area, like a capital city for example, you can use the traditional method of saving for a deposit and spending the next decade or five paying off the balance. For those of us who are not expecting to have a high-income stream next week, we need to look at the second option.

Saving
Your situation may not be as difficult as the one faced by aspiring homeowners in Australia, but it will serve as an example of the difficulty of taking the 'saving up' route.
The low affordability index rate today in Australia means it takes 8 years to save the 10% deposit on the average home, priced now at $850,000. (In Sydney it takes nine years.) During the time that our diligent savers have been putting away their $200 a week, they have been paying $500 - $900 a week in rent.

Let's consider someone from Melbourne trying to own their home. After achieving their goal and getting a loan, it will be another 25-30 years before they are no longer paying interest to a lender. Over the course of a typical home loan, the borrower pays about 80% of the total in interest payments on top of the principal borrowed.

All up, our hapless Melbourne wannabe homeowner stumps up $350,000 in rent and savings to have the $80,000 needed so they can borrow $780,000 and pay it back with an additional $625,000 in interest. All up payments for the deal, to buy their house is not $850,000 but $1,754,000, a little more than double what it's worth when they bought it.

Of course, inflation will cover most of that, probably, and at the end, it may well be worth more than the total paid, but probably not by much.

Sample of Income to house price ratio (111 countries)

Rank	Easy	Index	Rank		Index
1	Saudi Arabia	5.1	24	New Zealand	1.76
2	United States	3.4	25	Spain	1.74
3	Puerto Rico	3.1	26	France	1.72
	Not easy			**Very difficult**	
5	South Africa	2.55	29	**United Kingdom**	**1.57**
6	Denmark	2.43	32	Austria	1.51
7	Belgium	2.42	33	Japan	1.5
10	Netherlands	2.25	36	Greece	1.37
12	Ireland	2.16	37	Malaysia	1.34
15	Finland	2.03	47	Israel	1.11
16	Sweden	2.02		**Beyond hard**	
17	Canada	2.02	56	Singapore	0.92
	Difficult		57	Albania	0.92
19	**Australia**	**1.94**	58	Poland	0.9
20	Italy	1.9	80	Russia	0.57
21	Norway	1.9	81	South Korea	0.56
22	Germany	1.88	93	**China**	**0.45**

~~~

Saving Up. Yeah Nah.
42

"Saving is a very fine thing. Especially when your parents have done it for you." – Winston Churchill

If our Melbourne aspirants (and this applies no matter which state or country you live in) were to head off into the country for a few years, how would things turn out?

For a start, after allowing for a slightly lower income, more than made up for by lower living costs, they would own their home outright in 7 years just by maintaining the same saving regime, attaining the lower deposit goal sooner thereby saving rent for most of that time.

It is true the value of the home is lower than in Melbourne, but working on today's pricing, in less than 20 years (two thirds of the time of the Melbourne mortgage) they would own 5 houses outright by renting them out, the total value double that of the home in Melbourne that still has another 10 years of payments owing.

A lot will change in 20 years obviously, values and prices will fluctuate but because change applies equally to both sides of the equation, the principle does not change. The reason this works is because of the plateau effect. Stepping from 'no home' to a 'three quarter of a million-dollar home' is a huge step and takes many years to even save for the deposit. The much smaller step into the lower cost home means the debilitating effect of paying rent is halved, putting the buyer ahead much earlier.

In the 8 years it takes a Melbourne buyer to save an $80,000 deposit, a country buyer can own a home outright that is valued at nearly 4 times the amount of the deposit, some $300,000 plus an additional $46,000 in savings. If they then headed back to Melbourne and applied that to buying an average Melbourne home, they would own it in a bit over 10 years, 18 years after starting out, not 30.

Even better if they held off returning to the city for another 4 years as they would have $600,000 from the sale of two $300,000 houses. It would take just an additional four and a half years to pay off their standard Melbourne home bring the total time back from 30 years to 16.

This works regardless of changes in values, wages and inflation as all these things apply to both methods, so it is the principle that counts. The bottom line is that eliminating the cost of rent as early as possible pays huge dividends and smaller steps now are far more effective than one large step later.

Where?
Ok, moving can be daunting, but if you think you can't move from the city because you don't have a job, be aware that country areas need workers too, that the people who live in smaller towns and regional cities also work for a living so there is no doubt there are jobs available.

There are three different types of communities to consider, essentially regional cities, towns and villages. Capital cities tend to expand until they join up with earlier towns and cities close by, so living in the city can have different meanings depending on the area.

If the State capital is on the coast, you can count on the ocean-front real estate there to be extraordinarily expensive. The metropolitan area in all major cities is also expensive, followed by the absorbed outer-metro towns and cities. More affordable are the regional cities, regional towns and finally, the more distant villages.

Selecting an area to prospect for a future starter home can be a bit overwhelming, but it is worth taking time to look at all the potential locales. The overriding view needs to be that you are buying well to sell well. It's a well-known and accepted truism that you make your money when you buy, not when you sell. To begin to get prosperous, you should absolutely avoid thinking about the huge step from 'no home' to 'dream home'.

It's also worth remembering that you will tend to place more importance on either your home or your location. It is seldom the equitable 50/50. At one end we have people who don't care where they live provided the home is 'perfect' and there are others who would live in a tent, provided the location is 'perfect'.

Most of us are in between and it does not matter if you are close to one end or the other, the first house you build or buy is on behalf of a future owner, one who will pay you a lot of money to deliver their 'perfect' house. You are buying to sell, not to live in forever so don't pick suburbs with a reputation for being a slum or high crime area.

If you are buying in a housing development where all the land is of roughly equal value or desirability, you will be selling the house only, so your thoughts should be concentrated on how this prospective home could be especially appealing to a future buyer. On the other hand, if the plot of land in the development, is on a rise, has a view or aspect, then that is a significant benefit to add to the value and the house component is not as critical.

As we are buying to sell, to advance our future, where possible, try to select a block from the top 10% position-wise. Even more important, ensure the house is then in the top 10% in tidiness, gardens and maintenance. This not only ensures you get the best price but being in the top 10% is great for your sense of self-worth and a boost to your happiness.

Land vs house value
It seems obvious when you think about it, but there is a wide difference in the ratio of land to house value and like most things, follows the 80/20 rule.

At one end, we have the most desirable land, on the waterfront, in a beautiful setting, close to the heart of an internationally famous city. It is true the houses will be valuable but only because those who can afford the fabulously expensive land can afford a lavish house. How often have we seen a run-down cottage sell for millions because the land is so desirable? In this case the ratio is closer on average to 80% land and 20% house.

On the other hand, in a near rural village on the outskirts of a regional town, the average house is closer to 80% house and 20% land. Filing away this bit of information will help you in your decision making.

Selecting
The major regional cities of 200,000 and up are cheaper than the State capital but can still be expensive especially if they are within four hours driving time. Large towns and small cities on the direct connecting roads to the capital are in the next general price bracket down.

One method is targeting the smaller regional towns on the roads that connect to the highways that lead to the capital. These towns present the best opportunities and I categorize them with the none-too-flattering name, 'on the road to nowhere'.

What I mean by that is if you look at large coastal cities, there will be two highways running roughly parallel to the coast and at least one heading inland. The real estate near the highways running close to the coast is the most expensive, with the inland road being significantly cheaper.

In between these roads, are the towns 'on the road to nowhere' where you can buy a house outright for a couple of years wages, half the cost of one in a regional city. The same applies to major cities inland and across most of the USA for that matter.

These towns 'on the road to no-where' are still close to the major cities and their facilities, but come at a fraction of the cost of a city home.
In a good suburb in the State capital, not only could you not buy a house at that price, the house price in the smaller town, would barely cover the deposit. This is the best deal because they are still well within the Capital City morning-drive radius.

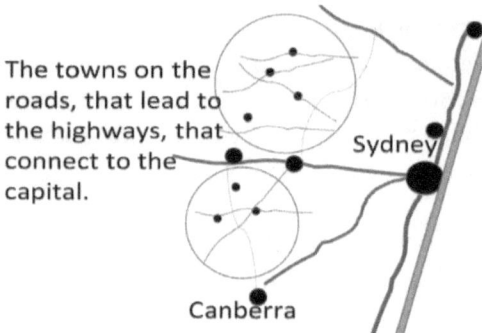

This is just an approximation and there are many other ways to choose a location and countless variations and opportunities. You can also use the circle method by putting a circle around towns and cities on Google Maps (use a free on-line app) with a diameter that suits the area. Villages within 20 minutes of a regional city or large town can be chosen this way too. You can check out the surroundings with a street view to get a feel for the area before leaving your comfy chair.

Whether it's the two-highway method or not, select towns that are not directly on 'through-roads' but concentrate your search on towns between or connected to these 'through-roads'.

In the UK and Europe generally there are very large cities spaced across the country and these guidelines need to be interpreted to suit the environment.

A similar situation applies in the US but with a considerable variation between States. There is some benefit too from the feel of living in a community, often hard to find in the city, but each to his own in this regard.

~~~

A Plan
43

"Life is either a daring adventure or nothing at all"
– Helen Keller

Albert, my imaginary friend, lives in the country, a place in my imagination called Titsupp Downs and he has always lived there. Of course, it happens to be in the zone we described, within a morning drive of the capital, less than 30 minutes from a small city and not on the direct through road.

For those of us who live in the cities, moving to the country for a while to get some capital together can be a formidable challenge. A plan starts with searching for a job in an area where houses and land are cheaper. This means some 'research' (in the popularized meaning of it) and may mean going there on a few days off and asking around.

It will not be where you live the rest of your life, so it doesn't have to be perfect. This is just a temporary stop on a long journey. When you do get a job away from the city, you are only there to gather your resources for a return bout if you still have the desire to live with the masses. The next time you live in the city, if indeed that is what you then desire, it will be to deal in property, to have others who don't know how to get prosperous, pay rent to your enterprise.

Once you have secured a steady income in an area with naturally lower costs, look to sell some of your surplus time. I know this is strictly speaking, part of increasing income but it is connected by more swiftly reducing your debt, especially the debilitating credit card debt.

I've never been able to find a satisfactory excuse for not using my surplus time, particularly when there are so many willing buyers.

As we have already discussed in the chapter 'Hiding Your Light', spend time on You Tube learning new skills. These are real money spinners as there are people within a few hundred metres of you right now, that will pay you to do these things for them. An advert on a local Facebook group, especially in country areas where there is a more 'local' feel, will always produce results.

How to buy, land or house (or anything major)
We all think we know how to do this. You look around for something you love and can afford and put in an offer. Maybe there's a better way.

This is one occasion when you must think of yourself first and be tough. Not just on the sellers but on yourself. Do not buy what you love. Nothing is forever, even rocks change a little each day, so what is your special 'I love this place' today, will not be so special tomorrow or next year or certainly decades from now. Buy with your head.

There are a few times when this does not work well, when buyers exceed sellers and this is a bad time to buy anyway. You would normally only be buying when everyone else is buying, if you desperately need a starter home or land. That would be unfortunate timing but you work with what you've got.

Assuming normal times (unlike the buying frenzy in some countries during the Covid pandemic) select three properties that fit the need and write down a price on each that would be a bargain or at least would make you very cheerful.

Put in offers on all three (subject to a satisfactory inspection or some other broad condition) and let owners know that you are making an offer on two other properties.

Even supply the addresses to show you mean business if that's what it takes to get them to the negotiation. Whoever agrees first gets the sale. That way you don't care which offer is accepted. Nearly always, someone takes it up, or at least makes a counter offer closer to your number. You always get a suitable property for the right price, if you are not being ridiculous in offering low ball.

Do not be bullied or manipulated by agents insisting that you can't make an offer without putting down a deposit. This is simply not true. Nor are you committed to buy, just because someone agrees to the price, so no, you won't be forced to buy more than one property.

Clearly you have indicated that you have not made a decision or have 'intent to contract' by advising you are making offers to others. The 'intent to contract' is one of the basic elements of a contract.

Property is no different to any other object for sale and no one ever passed a law to stop you from making a verbal offer. You can make an offer any time to anyone and you can change your mind provided you have not indicated 'intent' to contract.

When selecting land, a suggestion is to avoid flat open farming country to give you the best re-sale value later. We humans seem to prefer to live near a few hills and trees, although like all general rules, don't be pedantic about never looking at anything that doesn't fit some narrow criteria you have adopted.

If you do want a rule to go by, make it your policy to never make an offer on a single property. Say "I always pick three and offer an amount that will make me happy". You don't want to suffer buyer's remorse because you bought with your heart and it turns out to be disappointing.

Before looking at land, have the smallest possible budget in mind as re-sale is influenced more by the building than a marginally better location and remember, you make money when you buy well, not when you sell.

Recommendations/takeaways

- If you are tired of trying to save, escape to the country.
- Move to an area where you CAN afford to buy a house.
- Make sure that town is within a morning drive to the capital or major city.
- Get a local job.
- Best to buy a fixer-upper and improve it. Buy, improve, sell, repeat.
- OR
- Buy land and build your own house. (See next chapter.)

Sell it for a profit and repeat, moving to a more expensive area, whatever.

~~~

Build Your House
44

"A true gentleman is one who can play the banjo. And doesn't." Like so many witticism, attributed to – Mark Twain

Do you think these two statements mean the same thing?
"I can't play the banjo."
"I never learned to play the banjo".

Even though both are probably true (definitely true for most of us) the first statement is a negative, end of the matter, subject closed.

The second is a statement that merely explains the past, but hints at an entirely different future.

Are you tempted to say that you can't build a house? I disagree. Builders don't build houses, they organize and schedule trades, like a conductor of an orchestra organizes the musicians. Just about anyone with a modicum of organizing ability can build a house. All you need is some knowledge. You don't even need any inherent skill, although it would be helpful obviously.

By far, most builders are single-trade people who have learned the new trade of business. They have evolved into professional managers who organize other trades. Building involves many trades and I doubt a single builder in the country, could legally carry out all the trades, in even the most basic home.

To build a house, you need to be an organizer, not a builder. Obviously to be successful at building houses **for other people,** one requires knowledge and skill, not to mention prodigious business acumen and a license. Don't for a moment underestimate the business skill required to be a professional builder, nor for that matter, underestimate the massive costs involved in organizing a construction on behalf of a customer. In most cases, the builder is worth every cent.

At its heart, the job is about meticulous attention to detail, discipline, dedication to learning at least the basics of trade skills, willingness to take professional advice and self-confidence. All of these are within the grasp of almost anyone and you are most likely included in this group, so no, I don't believe you 'can't build a house'.

Will it be difficult, frustrating, frightening and seemingly never-ending? Yes probably, but now we are the type of person who focuses on results, not methods, aren't we? The time will pass just the same, whether you build yourself a home or not.

Why build? Why not a home/land package?
Spare a thought for the motivation behind the encouragement to go this way. Who stands to profit by your purchasing a package, making it as easy as possible? The builder obviously, the land developer and the finance organization. Especially the finance people with whom you will be in bed, seemingly forever.

Think about the components of a home/land package. These include the cost of land subdivision into allotments, streets, power, drainage, sewage and a profit for the developer. Before building can commence, there are Council approvals, soil tests and engineering costs. Up to this point, the percentage of the total that can be allocated to profit is probably less than 10%, maybe much less.

To break it up into the basic parts, let's spend $400,000 for a house and land package. The land is say $90,000 and the profit for the developer and the contractors who did the subdivision is $10,000. There is no way to avoid paying any of that.

Getting ready to build, approvals, designers, engineers and tests will be let's say, $30,000. Materials for the home $100,000 with a mark-up of say, $30,000 added by both the builder and on materials supplied by tradespeople.

Labour for trades across the board is commonly roughly equal to material costs although in some trades, plumbing for example, the labour is substantially more than the materials and in glazing, significantly less.

This simple chart is not intended to be a comprehensive assessment of housing costs in the mid 2020-2030's but the split is close enough to be a reasonable guide.

	Builder	Owner builder
Land	110,000	110,000
Pre-building costs	30,000	20,000
Materials	100,000	70,000
Markup	30,000	0
Trade labour	100,000	60,000
Builders profit	30,000	0
	$400,000	$260,000

Obviously there is a wide variety in desirability of certain areas, proximity to capital cities, beaches and other factors that affect land cost. A word of explanation about the figures above.

Pre-building costs can usually be shaved quite a bit if you are proactive in dealing with engineers and able to do a lot of drawing and planning. The main thing to remember is that this is just somewhere to keep the rain out and a step up the housing ladder, so keep the design simple.

Materials purchased by tradespeople are not negotiated down too hard, nor do they shop around for the best price, well not too hard anyway, because the tradie is not paying the bill, you are. It is amazing the cost savings when you need to reach into your own pocket to pay for materials.

When you are self-building, a very large amount of the donkey work can be done by you and most tradespeople are happy to avoid the crappy work and let you do it.

There are few nifty benefits too and one of those for UK self-builders who get a refund on the Value Added Tax on the materials, which is a damn fine thing.

Where all this can fall over however is failing to stick to the budget and opting for upgrades, afterthoughts and the tendency to build a 'forever' house, when all you should be doing at this stage is kissing the landlord goodbye. The cheaper the build, the quicker the result. You can build your forever house next time.

The Art of Building Overview
Choose land in a suburb you can afford, for sure, but it is also worth checking out the cheapest block in the 'too expensive' area. In general, 'good suburb' is better and 'good block' is better but not the most critical because you will be selling the house and you have a lot of control over its desirability.

As with the general advice in the previous chapter about buying property, make several offers and make sure the vendors know you are making offers. The first that accepts is the winner and that way, you know you are getting a bargain or at least a very good price and you don't care too much about which one you get.

The following is not a building course and the internet is awash with information on how to do specific tasks, but it's handy to have an overview and a word to the wise about what to look out for and what you will need to pay special attention to.

Everything you read from here on is general information and you will find that some of this is no longer accurate and most definitely is not an in-depth guide to Owner-Building.

Expect this to happen as you do the investigative work for your particular area. There are many Local Councils and Authorities, changing rules, local customs, strict enforcements and rule benders, so you cannot rely on the following as hard and unchanging fact. It is a guide to the matters you need to think about and investigate.

License
In just about every jurisdiction, you will need to do an Owner-Builder course for the State or area in which you live. Generally, this is not an onerous task and relatively cheap and usually, done online.

Designing/extendable
The object of the exercise is to get rid of the landlord so this house only needs to achieve this goal. It would be a mistake to attempt to build a mansion or a 'forever' home. There are a lot of simple designs available and there is no need to re-invent the wheel.

A three-bedroom simple layout will appeal to a wide range of future buyers and your design should reflect that. You are not building for you, you are building to rid yourself of rent and move on to the next stage.

When choosing a design, think about how much money

it will take to own it and if a single bedroom is all you are likely to afford without borrowing money, then do that but ensure it will be easy to expand as funds become available.

~~~

Part Six

Enjoy the Sweet Life
~~~

Albert Visiting Family
45

If there is one thing that Albert and Neerlee do well, it is enjoy life and part of that is staying in touch with family. I promised just a glimpse of the Dunning-Kruger family and that is all we have room for, but I see many elements of a sweet life in Albert. His optimism, generosity towards others, the recognition of friends that come in two types and the special care we need to take to conserve our resources above all.

Yes, it's true, clinging to his 1973 Leyland P76, looking for bargains where none exist, the total absence of ambition, these are exaggerations of an imaginary man, but hopefully Albert serves to underline matters we need to seriously consider.

Half the fun is planning and my claim is that Albert planned to drive to Brisbane and further, I claim that this is what he told me. Would I lie about that?.

"Right up to the minute we were leaving, I couldn't find my Gregory's and I was in a bit of a panic. Neerlee reassured me there were plenty of signs to Brisbane and once we got on the road, we could buy a new one. Anyway, our 1980 edition was probably getting a bit out of date now.

I don't know how some of these youngsters get a job frankly. After asking the young and clearly puzzled young lady at the service station where I could find a 'Gregory's' she finally worked out I wanted a map so I could find my way to Nudgee, which as I carefully explained, was in Brisbane.

When I got back to the car, I told Neerlee that the crazy girl just kept repeating "ya gotta have jeeps onya phone". She even tried to tell me how to spell it and still got it wrong. My dad used to drive Jeeps during the war and dammed if I can see how buying a Jeep is going to help me find Nudgee Road, let alone more than one Jeep.

While I was planning our next move, my ever-resourceful Neerlee Faithful spotted another car in the parking bay, a guy with an old but shiny 1972 GT Falcon which is obviously not as good as our later 1973 model Leyland P76, but he might have a directory he would sell us. She said she would go over and ask.

After about 15 minutes, Neerlee returned triumphantly, Gregory's in hand. Apparently Gregory's are now a collector's item and he wanted $20 for his copy. She not only managed to haggle him down, he gave her $50 and the book as well. Honestly, she should negotiate for the United Nations she is so good at getting her way. Anyway, the guy must have been crazy because he told

Neerlee his old GTHO Falcon was worth a million bucks. Can you imagine that? Probably just envious."

~~~

After Neerlee worked her magic negotiating skills and procured a Gregory's Street Directory, Albert told me, they finally made it to Nudgee and surprised the Andersen family.

Albert and Neerlee's second daughter Canbie Faithful, is married to Angus 'Aphid' Andersen. I've never met him, but they tell me Angus is average, in every way, average height, average looks, average weight, wears average thickish glasses, not bottle thick, but thick enough that his eyes look larger than normal.

His head is round, though not bald, rather more like scattered bean sprouts that have gone brown and limp from lack of nutrition. Angus has a fondness for flip up sunglasses which, indoors, when combined with apparently magnified eyes, makes him look like an aphid.

They have twin sons, Albert's grandsons and according to their probation officer, are special cases. This makes Albert very proud.

Strangely, they don't look at all like 'Aphid' Angus, more like their uncle Tall Terry or maybe his mate Toad. According to Albert, it's just great to see the family resemblance. They are short, squat, some would say rotund, strangely close eyes and have more than a passing resemblance to Freddy Kruger.

The fact they never remove their backward-facing caps doesn't help.

Their probation officer never calls around mealtimes, some would say out of curtesy, but it's really because of his cutlery phobia and for some reason when checking in on the twins, always puts his chair against the wall.
He's a bit strange Albert said, but when he described them as 'special cases' he won Albert's affection immediately.

After promising to let them know he is coming next time, Albert and Neerlee pointed their trusty 1973 Leyland P76 with the cavernous boot northwards, back to the comfort of home on their little acreage in Titsupp Downs.

Poor old Albert, we can have some sympathy for his misreading of just about everything, but in our imagination, his idyllic holding in a small and friendly community doesn't sound too bad.

~~~

Pleasure and Happiness
46

"You won't find the town of pleasure in the state of happiness"

Perhaps the most pervasive misinformation with which we are misled is that pleasure and happiness are interchangeable terms, that one is a synonym for the other. This view is so common, a simple internet search on the word 'pleasure' will bring up almost exclusively, sites that are fixated on happiness and offering gratuitous advice on how you can get your share.

Understanding the difference between pleasure and happiness is fundamental to achieving a positive financial position. They are quite different things with pleasures available at every point, from the free to the mind-bendingly expensive.

People who are living a depressed life, marred by tragedy or malice, are still able to enjoy the full range of pleasures, gastronomical, sexual, shopping and entertainment just for starters, proof if any was needed that they are incidental to happiness, not directly connected.

I haven't yet thought of a pleasure that can't be had while living a miserable existence. In fact there are countless people who indulge in every possible pleasure, yet lead deeply unhappy lives.

Alternatively, although I'm not recommending it for a moment, I believe it is possible to lead a contented life with few pleasures, although I have no idea why someone would want to deny themselves pleasure.

So long as we understand pursuing pleasure is in no way connected to a joyful life and can be expensive, why not enjoy all the pleasures available, especially the free ones?

Low cost but deeply satisfying pleasures; parks, sitting down, walks, not walking, coffee, coffee-people-watching, riverbanks, deserted beaches, catching fish, watching grandchildren play, playing an instrument, singing in the shower, emotion-stirring music, I have but begun. There are literally hundreds of pleasures to be had, just for the sake of recognizing and savouring them, sifting, smelling, touching, these are merely a few of life's pleasures.

Happiness is a state of mind and pleasures are, well, pleasant, so we should enjoy them provided we do not rely on them and we can afford them.

It's easy to understand the confusion. Pleasure, by definition, is a very pleasing state and happiness is also a very pleasing state, so pleasure must be happiness.

(A duck swims and a fish swims, so by that logic, ducks are fish. There is a Latin logic called 'post hoc, ergo, propter hoc' roughly translated as 'after this, therefore, because of this'.)

If we confuse pleasure with happiness, it is little wonder that the pursuit of happiness often gets side-tracked by running out of money. Pleasure tends to be expensive one way or another and happiness is free, fortunately.

Like our other emotions, pleasure is relative, meaning that to experience it, you need something to which you can compare. It is unlikely you will feel the luxurious pleasure of 'cosy' in a favourite jumper on a summer's day. You need cold to enjoy warmth. It is true, that if you are thirsty and you like beer, that first cold one is a joy, however it is not possible to enjoy your tenth, even your second with the same intensity.

We enjoy pleasurable holidays partly because the location is different, in contrast, but we also enjoy getting back home because we miss some of the pleasures of home, not always appreciated because of familiarity. Just the simple act of sitting down can be a huge pleasure if you have been standing for a long time but pleasure is soon gone, so there is no point in searching for continuous pleasures.

Why is it so expensive? For a start, those that sell pleasure naturally want to make a profit, so that alone adds to the cost. Often there is a price to pay in addition, which can take the form of weight gain, hangover and on occasions, a court appearance.

If the pleasure has a big-ticket price tag, a new car for example, the additional costs are obvious. Pleasure simply does not live long enough to create a state of happiness and the weight of the additional overhead begins to engender remorse and resentment.

(It's true you can buy some small inexpensive self-gift you hang on the wall, one that gives you repeat sets of pleasure and if all the other necessary components are in place, it can stimulate a sense of happiness, but we are not talking exceptionalism here.)

It seems hard to reconcile, a contradiction, living a life denying oneself pleasures and enjoying life to the full. At first glance it is hardly an enticing prospect, denying oneself, more like one of those solitary religious extremists scourging themselves before an altar.

In reality of course, we are not talking about living a life without pleasure, more like sometimes postponing it. One also gets the benefit of intensifying the pleasure later, while riding the wave of smug self-satisfaction one derives from feeling you are tougher, more in control, more alert to circumstances than the mysterious and ephemeral 'Mr Average'.

I say this almost tongue-in-cheek, but there is more than a grain of truth to it. Pleasure can indeed be more intense after postponement but there is another benefit, way above merely experiencing a more intense and gratifying moment and that is the surplus money.

Postponing pleasure very often results in abandoning the desired pleasure altogether as one decides the urge is so reduced and the cost so high, it's a lousy deal anyway.

When you live comfortably, money in pocket, there is a certain devil-may-care satisfaction in spontaneously splashing out on some little pleasure, heightened because it is not the norm and you've got the spare cash to do it.

Once you have mastered the art of postponing pleasure, it becomes a most satisfying way of life that leads to having excess money which is a major component of a financially secure life.

Buy a bottle of wine to share with your partner once a week, occasionally pick up a takeaway, but they are the exception, not day-to-day expenses. As you get stronger, tougher, you can get a sense of your power growing, your ability to control your life. The better you can postpone self-gratification, the better mentally you feel too and the extra money means you have cash left over at the end of the week which re-enforces your self-belief.

One particular pleasure is worth singling out, or rather the excuse for one. A common mistruth is "my job is so stressful I have to unwind." Unwind is a word that has only been invented relatively recently. Before that, what you needed was sleep, not drugs and alcohol.
If you take what you see in movies as true life, every time a character has a serious setback or finds themselves in a stressful situation, he/she gets really drunk. Alternatively, the detective's job is so stressful, he gets drunk every night to 'wind-down'.

If you are already financially independent, swimming in friends, brimming with self-confidence and topped up self-esteem, sure, get as chilled as you please, but don't tell yourself you 'need to unwind' with chemical assistance.

The seventeenth century astronomer and otherwise brilliant fellow, **Jean-Jacques d'Ortous de Mairan** not only had an impressive name, but he would also have been familiar with shift workers. Not too familiar of course.

After switching his view from the stars to his garden, he had an insight that an internal mechanism governed the workings of plants, independent of light and darkness. His hypothesis inspired the study of biological circadian rhythms that we eventually discovered affects the lives of a great many living organisms, ourselves included. It is unlikely he made the connection between shift worker sleep issues and our biological clocks.

We have a 25-hour clock hardwired into our brain's hypothalamus and we constantly advance the time by an hour a day to match the earth's 24-hour rotation. We have become rather proficient at this so that it is relatively easy to change to a work-later shift but difficult to manage the opposite direction. Long haul passengers' experience with jet lag and re-adjustments for shift workers are two of the common side effects. It can take 2 or 3 days to arrive in synchronicity with mother earth. It appears the unglamourous solution is sleep, neither beer nor pot, after all.

Brain processing

Can you feel pleasure and happiness at the same time? Despite multi-tasking and intuition, we really cannot think of two things simultaneously, rather rapidly switching between thoughts. As pleasure is a perception, a thought, it can only be experienced while you are thinking about the pleasure. When you stop for a second or longer to think of something else, pleasure disappears until one either consciously returns to it or a stimulation brings us back to the perception. This puts significant limits on how much and how many pleasures one can appreciate in one sitting.

One of the few pleasures that can be recalled and stimulate happiness is when one remembers the effect on others of doing something worthwhile for them. Doing good for others, making some small sacrifice that was appreciated, provides us with pleasure, not only at the time but in recall. It also fosters a feeling of happiness when re-lived. The same can't be said for recalling the pleasure of eating a piece of chocolate.

Happiness on the other hand is a state of 'being' a contentedness that requires no thinking. It can be the satisfaction of achievement, which may have been a pleasure at the time, but it is the achievement that brings the happiness not the pleasure component. You may enjoy the anticipation and the setting out on an adventure and feel both pleasure and happiness, but the happiness comes from achieving the long-awaited moment, not the act per se.

Later in the day, the pleasure may be much diminished by tiredness or even boredom, but the feeling of happiness can still be there. It's easier to be less confused by accepting the generalization that pleasure is a short-lived experience but happiness is the current state of satisfaction with your life overall.

~~~

Home-grown Drugs
47

"How high can it be?" – Sir Edmund Hillary at the base of Mt Everest.

Happiness and pleasure are so different, we even produce our own distinctly different hormones, Serotonin and Dopamine, to deal with them. **Serotonin** could just as easily be nicknamed the 'happiness hormone' and **Dopamine**, the 'pleasure hormone'.

Dopamine

Dopamine is a hormone produced in the brain that has many functions including reward, motivation, memory, attention and regulating body movements. When it's released, it creates feelings of pleasure and reward, which motivates you to repeat a specific behaviour. Have another piece of chocolate.

Dopamine is a type of neurotransmitter and made in the brain through a two-step process. First, it changes the amino acid tyrosine to a substance called dopa and then into dopamine.

Your nervous system spreads it along four major pathways in the brain, using it to send messages between nerve cells. Too much or too little can lead to a range of health issues, some serious, like Parkinson's disease, others less dire. Unbalanced levels have been linked to being overly competitive, aggressive, poor impulse control, binge eating, addiction and gambling. And chocolate.

Drugs such as cocaine cause a substantial increase of dopamine in your brain. It should come as no surprise that this satisfies your natural reward system in a big way. As you would expect, repeated use raises the threshold so you need to take more to get the same high and acting to make your body less able to produce dopamine naturally. This leads to emotional lows when you're sober.

When a person mistakes pleasure for happiness, the pursuit of more 'highs' can be consuming and without exception, leads to disaster in one form or another, financial, health or in relationships. Craving more dopamine reward, which can be sourced in so many ways, including eating, sex, gambling, alcohol and many illegal drugs, can easily become addictive. Did I mention chocolate?

Dopamine is also released when your brain is expecting a reward. Mere anticipation may be enough to raise dopamine levels. Unfortunately, if you have been looking forward to a particular pleasure and it fails to materialize, it may intensify your desire to 'fix' the issue and increase the drive to 'get back' the pleasure, even if now, that is inappropriate.

Fortunately, Dopamine is non-selective in that positive actions like achieving a longed-for goal, also motivate us. You feel good when you have achieved something or when you have done something good for another. These too cause a surge of dopamine in the brain. Training yourself to select for these more difficult pathways demands so much more of us, but it also leads us directly to happiness.

Serotonin
Happiness can exist on a continuous basis partly because unlike pleasures, which must be compared with the immediately preceding state to be effective, happiness can go on using just memory as a comparison.

Serotonin is the hormone that stabilizes our mood, our feelings of well-being, and happiness. This hormone impacts your entire body. In humans, it's also a neurotransmitter of 14 variants, having effects on mood, anxiety, sleep, appetite, temperature, eating and sexual behaviour. It's main use, a rather unglamorous and mundane one in physical terms, is the gastro-intestinal function.

One of the charming aspects of the hormone is that approximately 90% of the total is located in the enterochromaffin cells where it regulates gastro-intestinal function. If irritants are present in the food, the enterochromaffin cells release more serotonin to make the gut move faster, causes diarrhea, even vomiting so the gut is emptied of the noxious substance.

Not much happiness here.

The remainder, the 'happiness' part, is produced in the central nervous system, where it regulates mood, appetite, sleep, including memory and learning. It's a growth factor for some types of cells, which may give it a role in wound healing. It is also known to regulate aging, learning and memory.

The part we non-scientists care about, stabilizes our mood, feelings of well-being, and happiness. Too little may lead to depression, elevated levels can lead to osteoporosis, which makes the bones weaker. Why does there always have to be a trade off?

When your serotonin levels are normal, you should feel more focused, emotionally stable, happier, and calmer. While it is true a few hardy souls can find contentment in resignation to one's circumstances, it takes a determination, a force of will and contemplation that few of us have the time or interest to pursue.

For the rest of us, good health, a secure environment, a home you own, a reliable income, respect, excess funds, in company you love or at least like, these are the essentials for happiness.

None of that describes the need of the fleeting pleasure of a drug or a shopping experience. It's a moment of perception, the period from first perceiving that your life is in a good place and when you begin to think about something else. If you are generally 'happy' it is because you re-call that there are several to many things in your life that have a positive effect and few that you consider negative.

As you summarise or consider these benefits, you decide that on balance, you have a contented life, you are happy. We generally think these moments will occur nose-to-tail, if we can just win the lotto. Not so.

There would be many moments that are unpleasant, on the upside, giving you contrast to appreciate the pleasure that a windfall could bring, but there is no destination called happiness. It is a perception that life is not unpleasant overall, the good events outweigh the bad.

~~~

Licking The Problem
48

It's a re-occurring theme throughout this book, self-discipline, because it forms such an integral part of our lives. It's vital in everyday life and in every enterprise from getting out of bed, to doing the shopping, going to work and looking after our loved ones.

(On the thinnest of excuses, I've even woven an unexceptional story about the benefits of self-discipline from one of my ardent fans in Titsupp Downs.)

It is critical to our friendships, our self-confidence, our money in and money out, our homes and our happiness. So critical, one could be forgiven for having the misconception that we would all be super proficient in this art, so mentally muscular we could crush a coconut just by thinking about it, but no, most of us find this exceedingly difficult. Some find it so problematic, they spend their entire lives hand to mouth, pay day to pay day, achieving little and having less.

We need to understand it, appreciate it and if not conquer it, at least develop our power to the point our self-discipline delivers at least some of what life offers.

It's not too much of a stretch to say that change by sheer force of will, is witness to the actions of a titan. It takes power, it takes strength, to exert your will over your lethargy, your apathy, your resistance to change of direction.

The Nature and Source of Discipline

It requires discipline to get ready for work on a cold winter's morning. Do you cite this as evidence of self-discipline, that you perform this act most days, winter or summer, rain or shine, going to a less-than-fulfilling job? It could be reasonable to say in most cases that fear of losing a job is the motivation, so is it then fair to call this 'self'-discipline?

Motivation and discipline are different things but easily mistaken for each other. Never more apparent is this difference than when circumstances undergo a dramatic change, like leaving the military or the retirement of long-term employees or losing a long-held job. The dramatic effect can be devastating to the mental health especially if the individual was blithely unaware that most of the discipline required to achieve the basic act of earning a living has been provided by a superior.

The motivation was fear of losing, the job, the income, the position, the rank, the prestige, whatever the perceived loss, the motivation was fear.

The discipline was provided by the fear. When the fear of consequences is removed, there can be a sense of relief, of ease, but very soon becomes aware that progress has now stopped and to get it moving again will require discipline of the 'self' variety.

So much of our lives is forced discipline, not just from a boss but from society and nature. Nature is the ultimate boss, the enforcer, the one who insists that you get out of bed each morning on pain of bursting your bladder or wetting the bed, which would make you rather uncomfortable, not to mention unpopular.

External discipline, from nature or society, is no more beneficial to us than sitting on the bus as opposed to walking that same journey. If you are surrounded by discipline being applied to you from other sources, this is a very good time to develop your power, to exercise your own discipline to become strong.

~~

As I said, the thinnest of excuses, but please meet Tiny Little, a girl with discipline in spades.

The Ferrills, live on Ferrill Rd Titsupp Downs. Cheryl Ferrill is a widow and has a grown son Wilden Ferrill who used to visit the Faithful girls. (By coincidence, the Woolly family who lived nearby also had a boy called Wilden.) Albert didn't like the way Wilden Ferrill looked, especially at the P76.

Unlike Tall Terry who wasn't, Wilden Ferrill was tall and thin. Wilden was wary about calling on the Faithful girls because Offin Faithful liked Tall Terry. A lot. And often.

Tall Terry didn't like the way Wilden looked, especially at Offin and Wilden felt that Tall Terry was by default, too close by far, to parts of his anatomy for which he had great affection and valued highly.
So when Wilden called, he had to find a time when Albert was out in the P76 and Tall Terry was somewhere else, so at least he could try his luck with Canbie Faithful.

When Canbie moved to the big smoke to take up employment 'with the Queensland Government' as Albert described her job in the last typing pool in existence, Wilden had to seek other love interests in Titsupp Downs, of which there were little. Literally. Except for Tiny Little, the only daughter of Mr and Mrs Little who weren't and they lived in Little Lane.

Like many country families, the road was named after them but it didn't rhyme so it was called a lane. Tiny was only nicknamed Tiny because kids are cruel and lack imagination. Well the ones in Titsupp Downs State School were anyway. Tiny was a looker by any standards and could have her pick of the local talent, had there been some from which to choose.

The only contenders aside from Wilden, were Dashing Donnie and Hollywood Bob as Wilden Woolly was too young to be a contender.

Dashing Donnie had an impediment, aside from chronic laziness, in that he could never find the energy to remember names. He managed to overcome this failure of self-discipline in later years. When his first marriage to Barbara failed, he married another Barbara. When that marriage too failed, he took up with a new girl called Barbara and his friends started to notice a trend, especially when they found out he was trying his luck with her friend, who coincidently shares her first name, when Barbara was out of town obviously.

Dashing Donnie is fond of his little saying, that a man needs a woman who is a tigress in the bedroom, a chef in the kitchen and a meticulous housekeeper. Even more important he says, is that they should never meet. He heard that somewhere, obviously, as DD never had an original thought in his life.

DD had even offered to show Tiny his collection of dried cow pats that looked like faces and although tempted, Tiny declined. I like to think that Tiny Little showed great judgement and exercised her self-discipline to an exemplary degree, which was also fortunate for Dashing Donnie. What are the chances of finding another three Tinies?.

Hollywood Bob fared little better. Even in his youth, he was of those men who are naturally good looking and fall in love easily, though first and foremost with themselves.

It's said that in later years, Hollywood Bob even turned Neerlee's head, but my dear friend Albert never had a bad word to say about anyone. The worst he said was that Neerlee may have turned Hollywood Bob's head a few times, but she didn't turn it nearly far enough.
He also said since they had been married, the only time he managed to turn Neerlee's head was when he ran over her cat so that probably doesn't count.

In any case, Tiny stood strong, never took the easy path and eventually struck out on her own. She married a very nice man from the city and moved back to Little Lane when her mum passed.
What a love story.

~~~

Habits
49

"Doing nothing is hard. You never know when you're finished." – Leslie Nielsen

As most of us struggle with self-imposed discipline, we develop habits that do the heavy lifting.

Force of habit is well named, in that habit is the force that drives us forward when our self-discipline is weak and betrays us. Without habits to push people off to work every day, a lot would end up on the street.

The lack of exercise of the self-driven discipline muscles puts us in a weak, serious and dangerous position. Sooner or later that weakness will be exposed.

Isaac Newton, that frankly weird genius who lived in the 1600's, was the first scientists to be granted a knighthood and his achievements are so profound, they form the basis of most of what we know today about almost everything.

While the country was in lockdown because of the 1665 plague epidemic (even he hadn't thought of antibacterial remedies, unlike a virus, the plague was a bacteria) he studied at home.

Frustrated by the limitations of mathematics, the 23-year-old nerd invented Calculus, as you do, not that he bothered to tell anyone for the next 27 years.
One of his ideas, for which he produced a mathematical proof, was that an object, whether stationary or moving, will continue to do so undisturbed, until acted upon by a force. It appears, that applies to us and our habits too, although providing a mathematical proof is unlikely.

I suggest to you that change usually occurs only when discomfort urges us to provide a force to overcome our natural apathy or lethargy. If things are not too uncomfortable, we tend to leave matters as they are, even if that state is one of mild poverty.

Change requires the exercise of self-discipline and aside from questioning how much is self-imposed or how much weight should be given to the 'self' component, one thing that helps us along is habit. Habit can take over the role of the 'self' part.

For example, once you form the habit of getting up at a certain hour and heading off to work, the easier it becomes. Even when job satisfaction plummets, the habit will sustain you, providing the support of an external force or motivation. Habit is holding you on course.

Just as the habit of going to work gave you the discipline to keep your job, the habits of making real progress towards your goals and a secure life, will provide the same support.

The habits you develop, shape your brain, rather than the other way round. If you repeat an action often enough, you will come to be owned by that habit and that can work for you.

For example, when you develop the habit of not looking for shortcuts, rather someone who takes satisfaction from the incremental, you begin to derive pleasure from the journey, you develop your power, just as a body builder develops muscle and enhance the pleasure of possession. You become your actions.

If you habitually look for shortcuts, you will find the allure of easy payments, credit, immediate gratification, take over your life, postponing the achievement of the goals you started out looking towards.

The 17th-century philosopher Blaise Pascal, who lived in a time when blind faith in doctrine was normal, argued that as scepticism and logic came to replace pure belief, for the religious individual, it was their frequent acts of prayer that sustained faith.

In other words, he observed that if you removed the habit, faith would diminish and may be replaced by scepticism and logic.

We find this same result in our secular lives. When you practice or form a habit, you will eventually become a product of that habit. This works to provide whatever outcome you desire. You will become a product of how you act, so if you habitually physically carry out the actions that lead to self-confidence, financial independence and security, you will become a product of those actions.

If you live according to the standard format of working a job and spending your income on personal pleasures, there is a line of thought that goes something like this, "people end up wanting what they get, rather than getting what they want" which is a kind of resignation to life being tolerable.

This alternative is not so terrible, life being tolerable and mediocre. For most of us, in the absence of knowing how to change that outcome, tolerable and mediocre may be the not-so-bad outcome.

If you want to be financially independent and confident, you will need to do more than work and spend.

There's a trick to it.
It's easy to say of course, "just develop good habits" but that is hard. It also takes time, anywhere from three weeks to five months to develop a resilient habit.

Fortunately, there is a little trick to making it easier. For anyone who has ridden a bicycle, the first thing they learn is to start in the lowest gear. It's very difficult to take off in any vehicle in a high gear and we are the same. Before you tackle something that is going to take a lot of self-discipline, pick a small, lower gear. Anything that is part of the task, take the smallest, easiest component and crunch it.

This is just like starting in the lowest gear and gets you moving. It takes less effort to keep pedalling than to start pedalling. Unfortunately, if you stop pedalling, you will fall off, as you know, but at least you also know how to make an easy start.

Big Jobs
The thing most heartening I've noticed about facing big jobs, is how quickly one can nibble the edges off to make it much smaller. No matter how big, it only has a certain number of steps and each has to be taken. It usually does not matter if the next one is taken today or tomorrow but if you take just one or two of them today, you will feel not only a sense of accomplishment, but the task will also look smaller tomorrow.

I read a book a long time ago that resonated with me. I forget the name but I always remembered the example given, which went something like this. "Do you throw your loose change in the rubbish bin or do you put it aside for small purchases?"

When you are watching TV, waiting for the interminable advertising to finish, you are effectively throwing away the loose change of time. It really pays amazing dividends to get up and take some small step just while the ad break is on.

If you apply this to every time you wait for something, you are not being extreme or consumed with frenetic activity, just casually, calmly, converting loose change into real spending power. The point here is that whatever small thing you do during this otherwise wasted time, is a small step to be taken anyway. This way, many of the smaller ones are done before you get to grips with tackling the job, giving you a genuine head start. As a bonus, you feel better, stronger, smarter. It's another way to bolster our self-discipline muscles and goodness knows, most of us need all the help we can get.

~~~

Wins
50

"When you lose, be gracious. When you win, same."

There is a way of thinking, a way of life really, that I can heartily recommend. I'm classified by the taxonomists as a 'Sorta-tite' a sub-group of the 'Australian Lesser Tightwad' species. We are principally known for our distress calls when our wallets are attacked.

The reason I identify as 'Sorta-tite' is that I'm not really tight, but by trying to get a bargain, trying to minimize my expenditure, I get more than the obvious benefit of having money left over, which is as we know, a vital ingredient in winning a sweet life.

I've found that each time I succeed in finding the cheapest or more efficient solution to an issue, the better I feel, having achieved something. I feel that I've done well and naturally, that is good to share. While one does not always have the opportunity to share this experience, it can be re-lived many times and I encourage you to do so. If you keep a list of things to do each day, winning items stay up for a few days to be re-called with satisfaction. The feeling of success, the positive feedback you receive, is a real boost to your mood.

Whenever I meet my like-minded friends, we take the chance to talk about our wins and losses. It often starts with "I had a bit of a win yesterday" and goes on to relate the circumstances. If we haven't seen each other for a while, there are bound to be other wins on both sides to discuss.

Of course, sometimes we just have to accept that the practical solution was to pay full price and get it done. These too get told and it's the telling of the story that binds our friendships, the sharing of our successes and failures over a cup of coffee, that is a genuine pleasure to add to your happiness store.

If you take my advice and start using a list every day, you will, by default be keeping a record of your wins and this is a brilliant way to boost your satisfaction. It is also the most underrated method of boosting your performance.

Every time you achieve something, anything small or big, every time you get a bargain, get someone on side that was being difficult, whatever, many things are achieved every day. If you keep a list of jobs for the day and review what you have achieved, you give yourself a boost, a pat on the back and a good feeling generally.
It is amazing how many little wins we chalk up in a day and by lunchtime you should be reviewing, talking about, thinking about all the things you 'won' in the morning. You should also recall one or two of the big

wins from the previous day and at least one big one from earlier in the week.

It doesn't take long before you are saying to yourself, maybe someone else too, "I'm doing well here, I'm chalking up wins left, right and centre". You are well on your way to getting that 'positive attitude' the self-help gurus rave on about, but this one is likely to be true.

As I write this, just this week a friend came over to borrow an auger to dig a hole in his back yard. He did me a favour by borrowing it.

Why? I feel good being able to help him. A few minutes into our conversation he used a familiar sentence starter, one we have shared many times, "I had a bit of a win yesterday" and then went on to relate how he priced a new fan for his car radiator and after some calls, ended up buying a second-hand one for less than a quarter of the price and how it was easier to fit than expected. He was a happy man, having had a 'win', being able to share it with me and probably can also share it with other mates over the next week or so.

The re-living of your 'wins' is strong reinforcement for a positive attitude. The following day, I returned a trenching shovel I borrowed from a different friend, a week or so earlier. He was able to re-live the satisfaction of saying to his friend (me) "sure, there's one in the shed. Help yourself" and for me, it was a great excuse to stop by for a coffee and a chat.
Maintaining this type of relationship is good for your happiness, so do not be reticent to ask your friends for

help. You are helping to make their lives better, happier too.

I had planned to tell you about the big construction job I took on at home, building a huge man-shed, while writing this book. In the end I decided it was not all that interesting but one matter was important. I did my friends a favour by getting them to come over and help me lay the concrete. They not only had my gratitude, I know it felt good for them too.

~~~

Unhappiness
51

"We either make ourselves miserable, or we make ourselves happy. The amount of work is the same." – Carlos Castaneda

It's a pity we are not taught happiness as a school subject. So many of us naturally fall into thinking that the work cycle and location are immutable, fixed for their lifetime unless something, not of their making, comes along to improve the position.

What causes depression?
From what I've read on the subject, the answer is "we don't really know". Sure, there are factors that seem to be causal, but there seems to be a dearth of hard evidence.

To quote the Beyond Blue Organization "we don't know exactly what causes depression, **a number of things** (my emphasis) are often linked to its development... a combination of recent events and other longer-term factors, rather than one immediate issue or event". This is not exactly enlightening. They go on to say typical examples of factors that are linked to depression are "...long-term unemployment, abusive or uncaring relationships, isolation, loneliness, prolonged work stress, low self-esteem, perfectionism, personal criticism, self-critical and negative attitudes, serious medical illnesses and drug and alcohol problems".

None of that is surprising, however many people with these factors in their lives do NOT get depression. In addition, many people with NONE of these factors, DO get depression and there is no evidence of a genetic family link.

One matter everyone seems to agree upon is that it is not, as I believed, simply a 'chemical imbalance'. There is no way that I would claim to know the answer but over many years I have met and pondered, the lot of people who have been affected by depression. While it may be coincidental, I've asked myself "is depression linked to having an ill-defined sense of purpose, lack of a major burden or undertaking?" because it seems surprisingly common.

Despite the simplistic division of people into just male and female, gender is infinitely varied, but to generalize, women and men have some basic programming built in.

Goals
Men are (generally/largely/often) programmed to get certain things done, provide for a family, build a home, provide security, take out the trash. When that is done, what then? Consider the ex-military, now without purpose, with work and possibly social habits that do not easily fit society, seeking out the company of others is a

similar situation or maybe self-isolating. Depression seems to be rife among the ranks of those who feel they have no purpose, no clearly defined mission or goal.

As the Boomer generation moves into retirement, it has become more common to find mild depression or melancholy in men whose only purpose in life is to travel around the countryside with his partner looking for the next place to visit, to 'experience'. Once the mission of initial assembly of vehicle and mobile accommodation has been achieved, what then?

Having arrived at yet another perfect off-grid camp site, what is there to do but sit down and look at the view, maybe go for a walk or a swim or light a fire? What is the point? What is the goal? What sense of achievement does this exercise impart? Is it too strong or morbid a statement to make that a man without a mission is a death flower waiting to bloom?

Is this different for women? How critical are clearly defined goals for women? My impression, without evidence, is that in the early stages of family life, if that is their path, clearly defined goals are just as critical for women, however it seems to me that once the immediate family have fled the nest, more general goals are fine.

Maybe there is no difference in goals or missions between the sexes but in any case, it seems to me that men need clearly defined missions or they tend to get lost.

Why are you alive?
We need contrast to appreciate pleasant circumstances. If we feel no urge, no purpose, no sense of things undone, how are we to avoid a sense of under-utilization or even worthlessness?
The question could just as easily be "why are you still alive"? If the answer involves listing all the tasks yet unresolved, projects incomplete, an urgency to enjoy every aspect of life, not just the pleasures, then these answers suggest an unlikely propensity for depression.

If the answer is the easy, glib response, "because I haven't died yet" then I wonder if that is a not a signpost that points away from the path that leads to happiness. I suspect that one of the elusive causes of depression, mild depression anyway, is the absence of a raison d'être. We all need 'a reason to be'.

Self-destructive Behaviour
One of the tricky barriers to achieving happiness is making self-destructive decisions and taking self-destructive actions. This is surprisingly common and affects a large part of the population to some small degree and for some, it can be a difficult mental health problem to put right.

If you are a naturally compassionate, empathetic and or passionate person, you may feel your emotions more strongly than others, but the downside is, if you feel unworthy, suffer from feelings of guilt as we all do occasionally, you may feel this more strongly too and that could be a problem.

There are many common acts and attitudes that can be

warning alerts to look out for. Some are holding a generally negative attitude, remaining in difficult or dangerously negative circumstances, indulging in behaviour that pushes people away, self-pity, chronic avoidance and procrastination, being excessively self-derogative insisting you're not smart enough, not capable or attractive enough.

The original causes of this behaviour are seldom, probably never, the holder's fault and may stem from childhood trauma, neglect, abuse, sustained criticism, and a litany of other negative experiences.

If you tend to be self-destructive, it is almost certainly not your fault. No one wakes up one morning and decides to be self-destructive and unhappy but once taken hold, it becomes an insidious habit that is notoriously difficult to break and abandon for good. The good news is that it can be done and there are professionals who can help get it done.

Not everyone with a negative attitude is self-destructive but even so, negativity towards everything is never on the path to party-time. Always finding a reason why something won't work and justifying it by calling it 'being practical' or automatically adopting the 'Devil's Advocate' role, is sometimes just a coping mechanism, getting in before someone else puts you down. It's a bad habit nonetheless.

Positive Masochism
There are two types of masochism and your ancestors indulged big time. One is smart and positive, which comes as a surprise to most of us.

Our brains make a lot of unauthorized changes. One of them is positive masochism, telling us that some annoying things that must be done, are not really all that unpleasant at all. Now that you've become quite good at it, it's quite fun, right?

It certainly helps the species go on if the individual does the unpleasant, unavoidable chores that keep the individual alive long enough to breed. The brain can turn less than pleasant chores like delaying gratification for a better outcome, into a masochistic pleasure from the act of postponing the reward. It makes it easier to bear the frustration and take effect after a modest length of time. Positive masochism helps us deal with delayed gratification giving us a slight sense of pleasure at our achievements in conquering our desires for immediate satisfaction.

Self-destructive masochism
This is the classic guilt trip effect where some people feel unduly guilty over normal desires as well as recalling past indiscretions, shame or hurt caused to others. This sense of guilt can create a sense of deserving punishment or at least one is not entitled to happiness. Acting to punish themselves, sometimes causing physical harm, or more commonly, acting in a way that sabotages their life, the actions can provide temporary relief, getting drunk for example but the underlying feeling lingers on and the damaging actions need to be repeated.

Just as the brain can turn positive postponement of gratification or unpleasant but necessary chores into a mildly pleasurable or at least satisfying experience, in self-destructive mode, the punishment or destructive act can become a mildly pleasing experience. It can form a pattern of self-destructive acts that not only need to be acted out, but the acts also create a negative pleasure in inflicting the pain.

The shame of the most recent act adds to and reinforces the feeling they are not entitled to happiness. While people in this trap can get a sense of control over their lives, it only works when inflicting pain on themselves or acting in a way that sabotages their happiness to which they feel they are not entitled.

While treatment is available from professional therapists, they caution that the habits of self-destructive actions is difficult to break and permanently eradicate, though it can be done and even if one is only mildly affected, it is worth considering some consultation. After all, this is one shot at life with one shot at happiness and everyone, everyone deserves a crack at the sweet life.

Dealing with grief
Almost every 'disaster' comes wrapped in an opportunity, a good thing or a better outcome. Admittedly, it is sometimes wrapped so well it is hard to find, but generally, opportunity is there. One can choose the option to be rendered useless or one can pass off the set back and pick up the next opportunity which will appear very shortly.

Only with death, is there no option. It is hard to see a positive in that event and it rarely 'turns out to be a good thing'. Death however, does not have to cause pain forever and there are controls, tools to ease the pain and depression, at least temporarily.

There are complex reasons why people sincerely **want** to feel the pain of the grief, however long-term pain and grief can hardly have a beneficial effect on anyone. In the period after a loss, we tend to think of the person at their best, usually also remembering mostly the good times, their most charming attributes. We feel the full intensity of the loss in this mode.

Sometimes, we need a break from the pain and there is a straightforward way to do this. Choose to think about the times when the person acted badly and times when their actions hurt you. Instantly the pain diminishes and although you have motivations to revisit the pain of loss, a sense of obligation for example, there is no benefit in living it 24/7.

You can take a break from the pain for a time, perhaps even for months or permanently.

~~~

Negative Actions
52

"There is not enough guilt in all the world to change a single second of the past"

Guilt is a destructive fraud. We are not even who we think we are. We tend to think of our body as 'us' but we are not our body. If you had your appendix, tonsils, gall bladder and part of one limb removed, would you consider yourself now only 90% of a person? Proof, if any was needed that our bodies are mainly transport.

This chapter talks about negative actions, actions that affect your mind in a negative way. It might seem strange, sitting right in front of a chapter that attacks the whole 'positive attitude' movement. This one is about your actions, the next about trying to fake it in your mind, trick or convince yourself of something that is not true. But we'll get to that shortly.

Even if we cling to the thought that our bodies are an integral part of who we are, some parts of the brain you have now, did not exist 20 years ago. You are not who you were 10 years ago, almost nothing is the same. You are a rough clone of your previous self, a series of brain synapse connections, many of which, if not all, have been modified since they were first made.

Further, everyone around you who is more than 10 years old is a new person. Think of it another way, anyone you remember 10 years ago is dead. The one you know now is an evolution, a renewal, a clone-like copy of the original and while most of what you see is similar, they are not the same and neither are you.

Almost nothing physical is original, only a relatively small number of cells in the cerebral cortex, inner eye lens and heart muscle, are originals.

If we are not our bodies, then what? We are what we think, what we remember and what we feel right now. That is who we are. Memories however, are copies of copies and regularly modified slightly by adjoining or overlapping memories, so they change.

Your link with your past is characterized by memories that are the copies of copies of memories passed on from your old brain connections. Hard for us to appreciate, but our memories are at best, little more than half true.

Memories have wear and tear from use and non-genuine replacement parts fitted. While the overall shape is similar, the reality is different and two people who experienced an event long ago will have markedly different ideas about what really happened. Both will be wrong.

The now conscious 'you' is an ephemeral construct, only alive when you are awake. At sleep, even the 'you' is temporarily dead in the same way that your computer screen is blank when turned off. What I look back to, is only similar to who I am now.

Only opinions and attitudes can remain largely untouched by time, so unless you are ashamed of your opinion or your attitude, what purpose is served by feeling guilty over actions taken by a previous iteration of you?

Nothing is changed by guilt, no matter how much regret we feel for uncomfortable things in our past. Guilt is hard to shake but it serves no purpose and does a lot of harm. I suggest you do all you can to avoid reliving memories of events that only create misery for the current 'you'.

Resentment
Being angry with someone for things they said or did 20 years ago is bad for you. Pointless too as that person no longer exists. They may have changed into something similar, maybe not, but they will have changed and there is a strong chance the burden of what they said or did, if they know about it, has weighed heavily on them and they have self-punished more than anything hating them now can do.

In fact, making it subtly known that you are still angry and resentful, allowing it to bubble up at the first hint of disagreement on any subject, gives them a reason to say, "enough, with the guilt on me and the self-pity. Now, you are the transgressor". They would be right.

Murder

Daylight can be bad for your mental health. For the eight thousand generations that our species has been viable as a separate line, daylight was used for finding food, tending children and maintaining shelter from animals in the night.

Our species inherited this from hundreds of thousands of generations of our human precursors, literally our ancestors.

Our basic instincts take at least hundreds of generations to evolve, if not thousands. The motivations of our subconscious, the urge or need to act a certain way is just as strong in you now as it was for your recent ancestors 50 generations, a thousand years ago.

For most of us, those needs are now met by society but that does not stop your instincts from expecting you, driving you, to act the same way. If you habitually frustrate those instincts, killing time, you act against yourself and affect your mental health.

If you frustrate your instincts by using daytime distractions, TV, video games, computer games, crosswords or social media, to kill or destroy your precious time, you are not in sync with your body or your sub-conscious. Being out of sync leads to issues, not least exposure to depression.

I strongly recommend a policy of rarely turning on a TV until sundown except in special circumstance, some world-wide news event or to see a single program of special interest but never for mere background noise or killing your precious time with mindless babble.

The idea of a successful person, sitting down, frittering away their lives on advertising dressed up as 'news' or day-time TV soap opera, or otherwise killing time, just does not compute.

There is a world on your doorstep that can provide all the distraction, entertainment, exercise and social benefits that TV, screentime and time-killing sedentary activities destroys.

Living in the junkyard
In my opinion, it is not possible to live a contented life, a sweet life, if one has limited ability to self-regulate. A total absence of self-discipline and one would spend a lifetime mostly in prison. Self-discipline is what makes us conform to societies demands and in turn, being accepted by our peers, our neighbours, our countrymen and women.

It is not saying too much to claim that an advanced power and strength of control over our desires, is the single most important skill we need for our happiness.

The way that people live is a good indicator of a person's ability to self-regulate. People can make very accurate judgements about you, by the way you maintain your surroundings. If your house and car are a mess, that is a bad sign. There are lots of easy excuses for living like an animal, leaving the mess and moving on or just lying in it and I'm sure you've heard most of them.

One of my favourites is "I do the specialized stuff and anyone can clean up, so I leave that to those who can't do what I can do" as if every waking moment was already allocated to 'specialized' tasks. The absurdity of that statement often comes into focus as they push aside the dirty dishes and settle down to spend a few hours watching day-time television.

Another favourite 'I like it this way' made lie by the same person insisting on a perfectly clean and tidy holiday apartment. Clearly, they don't search Airbnb for 'messy-holiday-accommodation' which strongly suggests they are lying to themselves and any visitor who sees it. "It doesn't matter how I live" is about as wrong as one can be. It matters very much.

If your property is littered with toys and rubbish and old furniture, dropped cigarette butts, old bits of pipe and building materials, old cars and gardens full of weeds, you have a serious problem.

These are not mere eyesores, much worse, they are mile markers. They are markers on a road you don't want to be on, a road to nowhere. The longer one stumbles over the mess, the more often the mess highlights your inadequacies and more one is driven to a sense of hopelessness.

When one surveys a house full of rubbish, unfinished projects, broken light sockets, incomplete maintenance, leaking taps and dirty dishes, the vastness of the task is so wide, there seems no point in starting. It is easier to pretend, easier to ignore the mess and go back to sleep or worse, go out and score/spend money to make yourself feel better.

You cannot earn enough money in a lifetime, if you can't get off the wrong road. Let the mile markers be your guide.

~~~

The Positive Attitude Scam
53

In one way, understanding this subject did help us win our sweet life, partly because it pushed us to see things for what they really were. Not being in the habit of pretending we could choose to believe or not believe something, meant we were less easily taken in or side-tracked by low quality ideas or seduced by justifications to buy things that we not going to help us get to our goal.

If you understand and embrace this chapter, you are far less likely to take paths that look enticing and easy, but are not going where you need to be.

When I was a lad, I was ambitious and I really wanted to know what to do with my life, what I should become, how to go about being successful. I actively sought every bit of 'wisdom' that was to be found, long before you could just Google it.

Like millions of others, I was caught up in a falsehood that persists to this day, the "Power of Positive

Thinking". It was called 'believing in yourself' and the secret apparently, was to 'believe' and be 'positive'.

It worked well, but only for the proponents. If you succeeded in your endeavour, won the game, made the sale or got the girl, it was because you 'believed'. If you didn't succeed, didn't win, it was because you didn't 'believe' hard enough.

With a sales pitch like that, you can't lose. If the sucker who bought the books and or the motivational tapes fails, it's his fault. It's never the proponent's fault.

Today, every second action movie has an example of the bumbling incompetent who is encouraged to 'believe' and at the end, goes on to save the day. Football coaches boast that their winning team 'really believed in themselves' as though they could flip a coin and choose whether to 'believe' or not.

I knew it never worked for me and for a time, I accepted the 'wisdom' that I did not 'believe' hard enough or didn't really try hard enough to develop a positive attitude, but even at that tender age, I was smart enough to suspect it was fake.

Well that turned out to be nonsense and the whole 'believe' and 'positive attitude' was nothing more than a misguided hypothesis, very much in the same vein as dieticians being advised to tell their clients to avoid eating fat to reduce weight.

That particular fallacy was merely intuitive, compelling and easy too. Science eventually demonstrated that aside from overeating, the primary culprit for obesity was easy access to and excessive uptake of high energy content food, carbohydrate in particular. At the time, it sounded right though, intuitive, don't eat fat and you won't get fat, which in hindsight is like saying 'eat brains and you'll get smarter' or 'eat heart and you'll be braver'.

It seems to me, pretty clear why the 'believe' and 'positive attitude' are in the same intuitive category.

One only has to consider that you cannot choose to believe something. You either do or you don't and it is founded on evidence (unlike faith which is founded on hope).

If the evidence is there, it is believable. If not, then no matter how hard you try, you just don't believe it. Not really, even if you say you do and try to convince yourself you do. If the evidence is absent or contrary, you do not really believe anything. That is a very good thing for which you should be grateful. It means you have an independent mind and are not so easily misled or victimized.

The same applies to 'just have a positive attitude', which is a glib way of saying,

"pretend you can do it, even though there is not a shred of evidence to suggest that you can." You quite reasonably believe your chances of success are minimal, but "you'll succeed anyway" if you 'just have a positive attitude'.

That's not to say there are not circumstances where the situation has never arisen and the person who attempts something after going through the 'let's pretend' process, actually succeeds. They were always going to succeed, no matter what they thought of their chances. Attributing success to the 'positive attitude' scam is plain wrong. For more on that, read up on the logical fallacy 'Post hoc ergo propter hoc'.

So, does this mean having a negative attitude will make you successful? That question is another logical fallacy called the 'false dilemma fallacy' where you are limited to two false choices. Accepting that you do not have a positive attitude towards a particular activity, does not mean you have a negative attitude toward it. One can reasonably sum up the chances of success in a practical and scientific way, without the mumbo jumbo of faked 'belief'.

A lot has been written about positive attitude and most of it seems to suggest that you can give yourself a positive attitude by believing that you can do it, whatever the significant 'it' happens to be.

According to sports and business wisdom, you can win, if you believe you can win because this gives you a positive attitude.

There was a popular theme doing the rounds years ago that went something like 'if you believe you can, or if you believe you can't, either way, you are right'.

Sorry, I just don't buy it. I have never understood how someone can choose to believe something. I understand how one can pretend to believe, how one can tell oneself that you believe, but in your heart, you believe or you don't.

I won't get into making a claim that the sport and business coaches are right or wrong, because I cannot provide proof either way. Neither can they of course because any results are anecdotal and there is no science that can demonstrate a guaranteed result based on an athlete telling themselves that they can win.

Many times they do and may assign the result to the little pep talk before the event but there is no proof this was the causative agent. It's self-serving too because if one does not win, it was because one did not believe enough. It all sounds remarkably like prayer and about as effective in my opinion.

I suspect we have a natural tendency to favour either positive or negative. I will provide just one anecdote that demonstrated to me at least, the opposite effect of a positive attitude, actually believing you can win.

I was playing squash in my thirties and one night I was scheduled to play a guy who was at the National level, way above my grade. I knew I had no chance, so did he and so did the spectators. My only thought going into the game was not embarrassing myself by not getting a point, a complete thrashing. I gave my opponent the impression in the warmup that this was going to be an easy victory for him, barely an effort, just going through the motions.

In my desperation not to look too bad, I played my heart out and amazed myself and the onlookers by winning the first game. I won the second game too and in the third and final game, with pounding heart and just 3 more points left to score, a fatal thought crossed my mind. I might win this.

The impact of that thought was devastating and I never took another point, going down a very respectable 3 to 2 games. That moment, that fateful moment, I thought the positive 'I can win this' thought, is forever etched in my mind.

Since then, I've seen the same thing in football matches, countless times as the winning side looks at the clock and says 'we will win this' that same gnarly, devastating 'positive' thought as the other team makes up for lost ground and goes on to win. The winning team was the one that was convinced they could lose, right up to the last minute.

This in no way should be interpreted to mean that I favour negative attitudes, especially as I am the owner of a healthy optimistic outlook. The point of this discussion and anecdote is that I have no idea how you change, if you have a generally negative view of the world, however I suspect 'generally negative' is not one I would put money on to lead to happiness.

If I were forced to pick a side, I'd say that people who are on the extremes of either side have less chance of being successful. Those who tend to be too positive, like me, tend to avoid the reality that things will probably not turn out as wonderful as hoped and the truly negative people don't bother trying as things are bound to fail anyway.

As my anecdote above persuades me, having an 'attitude' either way could be just incidental and/or have no real bearing on outcomes. I don't know but the scars from my loss have persuaded me to never believe I will win until I have the prize in my hand. Even then I look around in case there's been a mistake.

I for one, have no doubt that a smooth, sweet life, is about attitude first and foremost, while acknowledging that our environment, health, home ownership, friends, family and financial position are significant players in the mix.

With that thought in mind, it's worth recognizing too that nothing stays the same. Nothing in your life will be the same tomorrow, for better or worse.

Soon, this too will pass, for better or worse. If things aren't too bad now, appreciate it. If things are bad, they're less likely to get worse than they are to get better, so cheer up.

~~~

Matters of the Mind
54

It's a long time since I played piano professionally, but one of the songs I still like to play and sing is 'You're A Lady' by Peter Skellern (1947-2017) who was an English singer, composer and pianist. The song has a line that goes "Oh I **know** I could make you happy, so the things I have to say....".

While I love the way Peter sang it, I know that particular line is not true. No one can make you happy. That's a job, like going to the loo, you must do for yourself. (Truth to be told, even if it does support a false notion, it's such a great line, if I had his talent, I'd probably write it too.)

I guess, all other matters being equal, the difference between a happy life and the alternative, is accepting that one is responsible for their own happiness. It's not up to someone else. Obviously others can affect your current mood by action or omission, but over the longer term, we are all responsible for ourselves, our own happiness and with it, the chance to live a sweet life. There is no doubt that people can act in a way that will make you unhappy but the reverse does not apply. No one can make you happy and frankly, nobody will. This saves a lot of disappointment.

It's with this in mind, I've made a short list of things for which I take responsibility and I have three **States of Being (the three 'P's)** in which I find myself. I've noticed a distinct difference in my mood when I am in each.

Proactivity mode
This broadly is the mode when I'm actively pursuing a goal, focused on getting or achieving my goal. My mind is on maximum work-out. This could be preparing for a trip, building or creating, learning an instrument or just working on a home project. I understand the effect of this mental exercise tends towards lengthening one's life span. It also, magically makes one feel happier, the

subconscious knowledge you are doing something good for yourself and others.

Participation mode
This is the mode when one is working with others perhaps in a pastime and not necessarily willingly, to begin with anyway. While this is a less beneficial mental exercise than actively pursuing a goal pro-actively, it is still beneficial and helps many people hold off the grim reaper a little longer.

Passivity mode
There is a mountain of evidence that shows spending a lot of time in passivity mode shortens life.
Unfortunately, it is the easiest to lapse into, where one sits and watches, a mere spectator of life. I have no desire to waste a second so when I indulge in sitting still, it is the opportunity to think, to absorb my surroundings and or to enjoy the company.

If you find that you are spending a lot of time in front of a screen, especially un-natural daytime watching TV, videos, video games and the like, you are probably doing everything possible to reduce your happiness, decimate your self-confidence and promote the growth of depression.

It is even possible to feel you are not achieving goals when actively participating in your interests, be that playing golf, bowls or travelling. There is no doubt you are participating in something, far above merely sitting and watching TV but still, unless you have a specific goal in mind, sometimes, these activities are just not enough, not actually striving to achieve anything in particular.

Having clear goals seems to engender great protection against melancholy.

I was also very much taken by the idea of options when I noticed the impact that reading them had on me.

In the latter years, when struck by disastrous news in my business, which happened with tedious frequency, I learned to not break into a panic, despite the rush of penalties and life-wrecking scenarios that filled my mind. My first question was "what's the worst that can happen"? followed by "there's no death penalty for this is there"?

Because it happened so often, putting it into that context was the first and usually quite effective line of defence. Next I'd write a list of options, even if I could only think of one or two (can you have a list of one?). The act of writing it down pushed the thoughts about the mountain of fertilizer that was about to come crashing down upon my head, to the side for a few moments.

Inevitably, I'd find several other options to add to the list and by reading back over them several times, I'd feel a whole lot better about the situation. I was protecting my sanity if not my happiness first and foremost. For a time I became convinced that having 'options' was the secret of happiness, the key to a sweet life and I've not really moved far from that position, just fleshed out the full picture somewhat.

Aside from the practical assistance of reading back over my options, I gradually noticed that most, if not all past truckloads of excrement had a neat benefit, a nugget of gold, buried in the load. Naturally it was never sitting on top and occasionally buried so deep it took months or longer to dig out, but almost invariably, fate did not forget to pack the gold with the fertilizer.

I lost count of the number of times I said "well that turned out well in the long run.". I guess I could even put my greatest disaster in 30 years, the loss of my company, in that category. Not only do you have options that directly apply to the disaster, but you can also change location, change your main income or home, you can find new friends or partner, invest in something better. Don't get hung up on disaster. You will have a few more before you hang up your boots, so don't make like it's the end of the game. It is not.

It's true that more money can improve life to a very large degree but this is mainly because more money gives you more options. To have options, you don't really need to be rich but you do need to be aware that at every opportunity you should be thinking about creating an optional action to take, if things don't go well. Even knowing you have a few second-rate options gives a sense of security, a sense that things will not go badly no matter what the outcome.

The effect of seeing your options in print can have a profound impact. Relief, reduced anxiety, hope, many good things come from committing options to paper. Perhaps this is not immediate, same day happiness but it is the beginning and options will take you there eventually if you just give them the chance.

A Touch of Philosophy
55

It may seem unduly philosophical but we can learn a few important strategies from the past, in this case, way past.

Søren Kierkegaard (1813 – 1855) was a Danish philosopher, theologian, poet, social critic and religious author who is widely considered to be the first existentialist philosopher.

Much of his work deals with the issues of how one lives as an individual, giving priority to concrete human reality over abstract thinking and highlighting the importance of personal choice and commitment.

He proposed that individuals are solely responsible for giving meaning to their life, not others, society or religion, and they should live it passionately, sincerely, authentically. The traditional Abrahamic religious perspective is that we exist solely to fulfill God's commandments, which by default gives meaning to people's lives.

That is not the view taken by Søren who said the universe is 'absurd' which in a philosophical context, means that there is no meaning in the world beyond what we give it. The world itself does not have a meaning or purpose, it just exists and we exist as part of that. Anything can happen to anyone at any time and a tragic event could plummet someone into direct confrontation with the 'absurd' universe.

Clear thinking is a skill and it takes a concerted effort to put aside our prejudices, assumptions and desires for how we want things to be, to accept reality. Our chapter on friendship showed us that, reality is seldom what we want it to be. It makes it a lot easier to deal with misfortune if you see clearly they are inevitable and awareness that even gold does not come out of the ground pure.

We can use our clear-thinking technique to turn our attention to the smaller joys left exposed by the mauling of misfortune. Our happiness and appreciation of our lives depends on how we perceive the world and how we divide our time. We can think but one thought at a time so moments drinking in the beauty of a flower is time denied to wallowing in self-pity and misery.

Pre-decisions
In my basic training as a pilot, setting out one's options

before making the flight was drummed into me as if my life depended on it. Which it did. Mountains hide in clouds so when flying into dubious visibility, we were trained in pre-decision making.

What this meant in practical terms was that you decided to take a specific life-saving action, such as turning around or diverting to a safe area to land, when you reached the pre-determined point or pre-determined time.

This removes those vacillating, 'wait a little longer to see if it improves' life and death decisions. The optimal time for making decisions that involve accidently dying is not when under stress, so we trained to make them when we were safely on the ground, before we left. This turned out to be very useful in every other aspect of life.

Whenever you have chosen a course of action about which you are feeling a bit twitchy, make a decision now about what you will do at a given point, to make a drastic change, abandon the effort, invest more, whatever, but make the decision now not when you are under stress.

It has the additional benefit of relieving anxiety about the future of the project as though someone else has already made the decision and all you need do is sit back and wait to see which one is selected.

With decisions made in advance taking the pressure of having to come up with solutions on the fly, I have a little emergency supply of actions I find maintain my sweet life and I recommend them to you. I really do use them quite often.

Act Happy
Regardless of how you feel at the moment, if you act a certain way you start to feel that way. Our mental state and our physical state are so closely linked that each affects the other. Many think that it is one-way traffic, that only if your mind is happy, you will laugh and smile. It's as though our feelings are being pulled along on a string.

The truth is it works both ways, more like our emotions and our actions are connect by stiff rods, each effecting the other. You only have to act a certain way for a short time and pretty soon, that's how you will feel. People who laugh a lot, live longer too.

Asset Stocktake
Take a mental stocktake of your assets. If you regularly look back over what you have, you are reassuring yourself that you are making progress, that there was a time when you had a lot less and this tends to bolster your mood.

Family and Friend Stocktake
Take a second stocktake, this time of your family and friends list, how many are alive and pleased to talk with you. You are not alone in this, there are people you know who will stop for a chat if you just make the effort to say 'hello'.

Do Someone a Favour
Offer to help out. This is a big one, powerful. We evolved an instinct to help others which in turn gave us protection from an uncaring natural environment and still today we get a boost from helping others.

Helping someone else is essentially a selfish act in that you are often the biggest beneficiary, receiving the massive boost of Serotonin you brain rewards you with for doing something smart.

Call someone for their benefit
Call to listen to what they have to say and make the effort to NOT talk about your own life. Resist the temptation to talk, listen. No one ever calls exclusively for your benefit, so this may be the only call they receive in a very long time that asks nothing of them. You will feel more powerful for having exercised your self-discipline muscles. Better than a gym and you will enjoy the Serotonin hit too.

Chase a bargain
We all love a bargain and so long as we curb the desire to buy something we don't really need, this is a really good booster shot. It only works if you spend a fair bit of effort in finding the best deal possible (without doing the wrong thing of course) and only if you had to buy it anyway. Talking about it with your friends later is a second shot too.

How Are You?
When someone asks, tell your friends that you feel happy. Don't settle for "not bad" "yeah, pretty good" go the whole way and say "to be honest, great, things are going very well these days, couldn't be happier", so long as that's true of course. Mostly it should be so don't hold back. The more you talk about it, the more you become it. Why not, you have a lot to be happy about.

Planning
There is no doubt that planning in some cases turns out to be more fun that the trip, so spend plenty of time planning holidays, especially very short ones. Plan and take a lot of short trips, they are often more memorable, more fun than the 'big adventure' trips. Your mood gets bonus points if the trip is cheap or free. Public facilities are good targets for these.

Projects
Without doubt the most important booster is having a lot of projects on the go, so much so that you barely have time to fit them all in. Create a purpose or major undertaking that will take months or even better, years to achieve. A second or third language, a substantial construction project, write a book, become a touch typist, learn the piano, the list of possibilities is endless.

In Summary
Regularly revisit, re-read and revise your knowledge about your options and your wins, take some self-discipline exercise every day, make an effort to appreciate how far you have come and work on your projects. Make these your favourite habits and you will live a happy, sweet life.

~~~

Epilogue

Well now we come to the end of my collection of tools I believe helped us get our lives back in short order. The journey was much like having the chance to live your life over, but equipped this time with all the tools and knowledge it takes a lifetime to discover. Even then, most of us don't get to understand it all, just as I'm sure there are very many other nuggets that could have helped us even more.

If you've had the tenacity to see this though to the end, to see things through my eyes and the eyes of my imaginary family the Dunning-Krugers, I think you are now as well-equipped as I, to achieve the sweet life, probably better equipped, as you are almost certainly younger and have more time to realize the benefits.

I know for sure, that had I known all this forty years ago, even 20 years ago, my life would have taken an entirely different trajectory, for better or worse. I would certainly own a lot more property and that may not directly translate into happiness but as we discussed at the beginning, it's a lot easier to be happy if you have the money.

If happiness is a destination, although we can agree it is not, then paradoxically I have arrived, however I'm well aware that living a sweet life, day to day, revelling in the joys of life, it's like standing on a ball. It takes practice to maintain one's position and composure.

Take and make of this what you will with my best wishes for a successful, contented life.

My final word is that life is a cellar that won't be restocked. It diminishes, one by one, day by day. Only as the last few bottles are opened, do we really begin to appreciate, how unique and wonderful each one is.

But we don't have to wait until the racks are nearly empty. Love today, for it too is unique and won't be tasted again.

~~~

www.ingramcontent.com/pod-product-compliance
Lightning Source LLC
Chambersburg PA
CBHW020315010526
44107CB00054B/1857